USA

God bless the USA, so large, so friendly, and so rich.

W. H. Auden

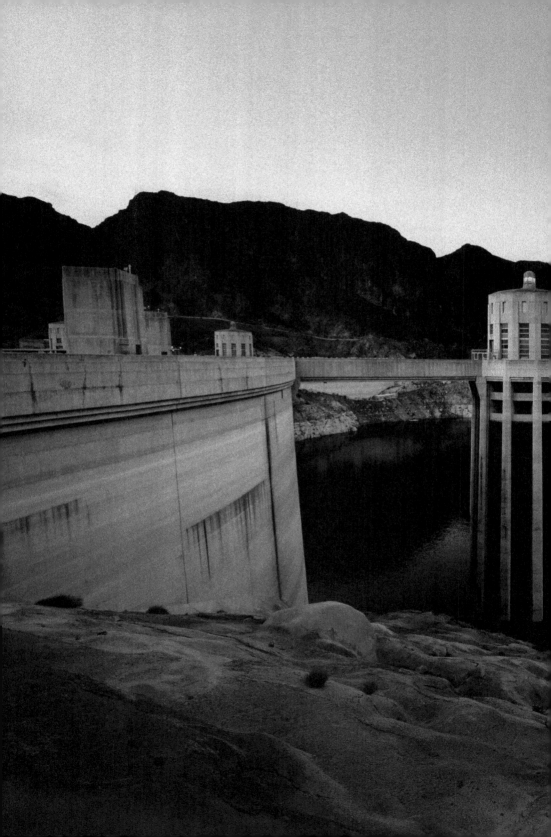

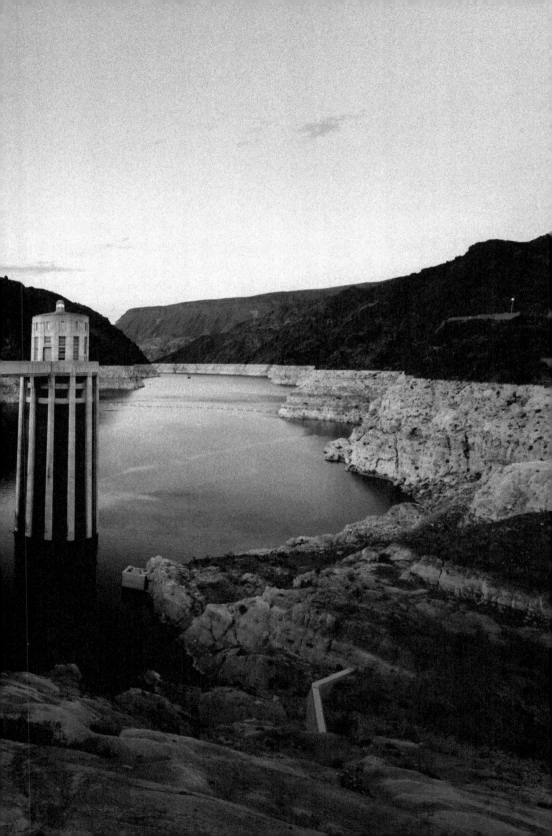

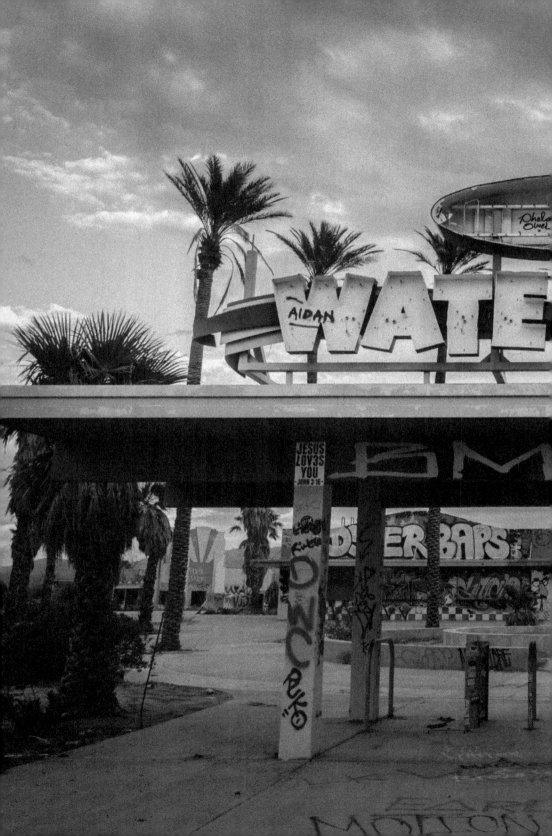

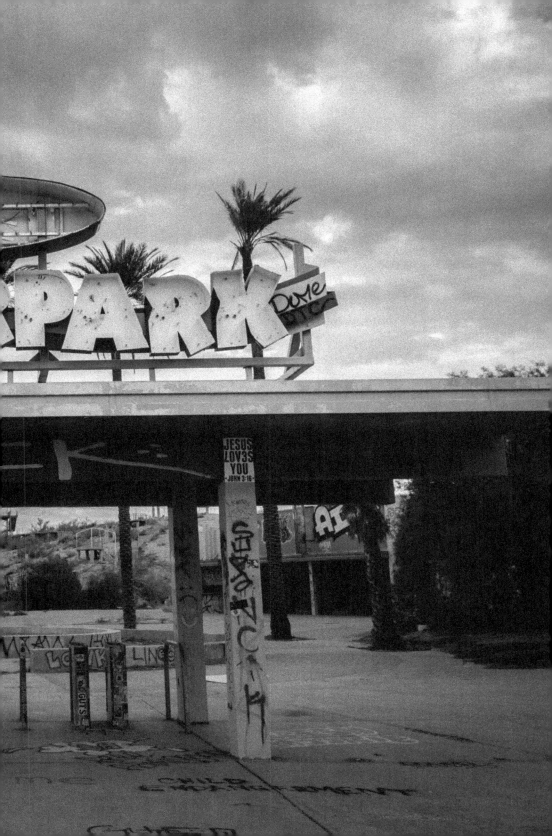

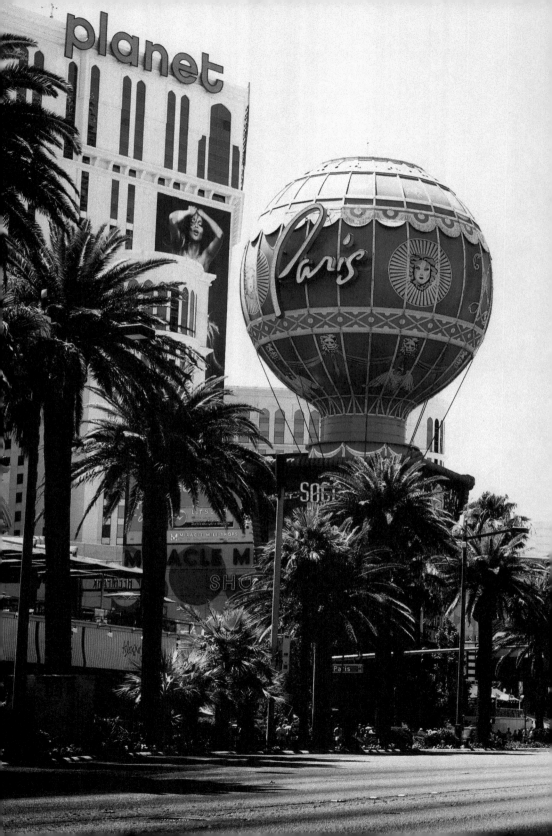

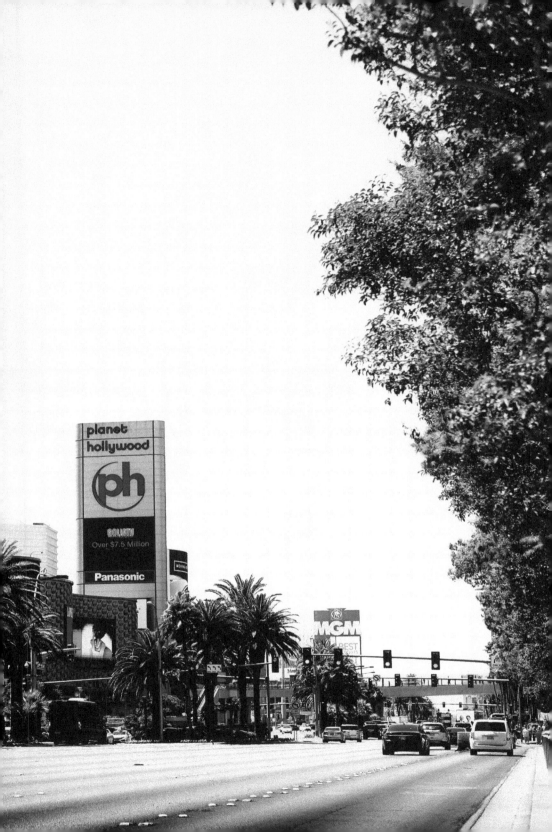

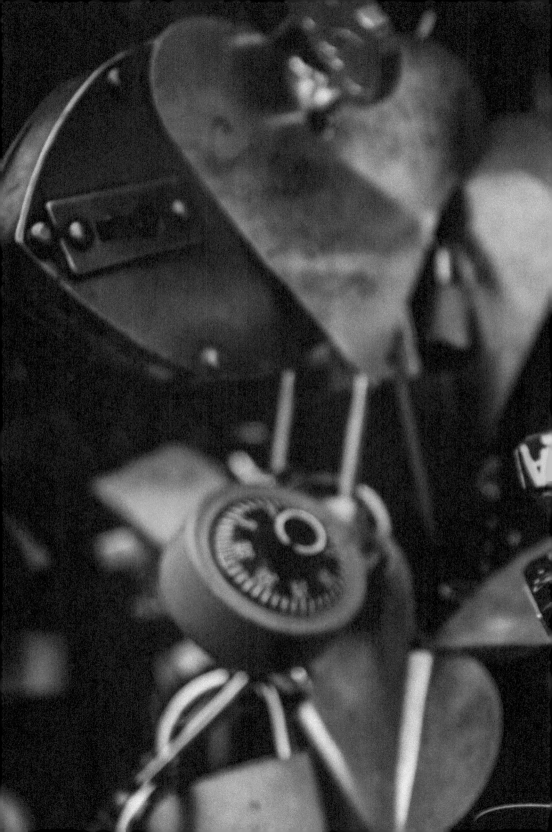

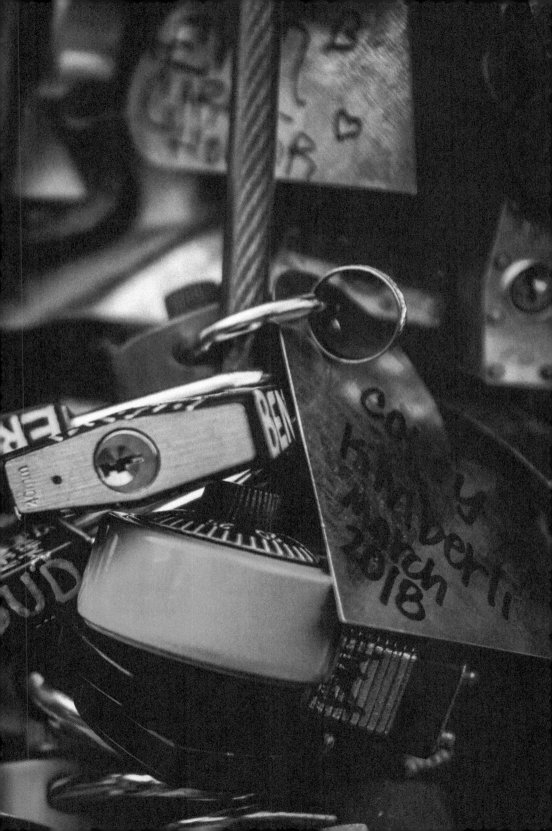

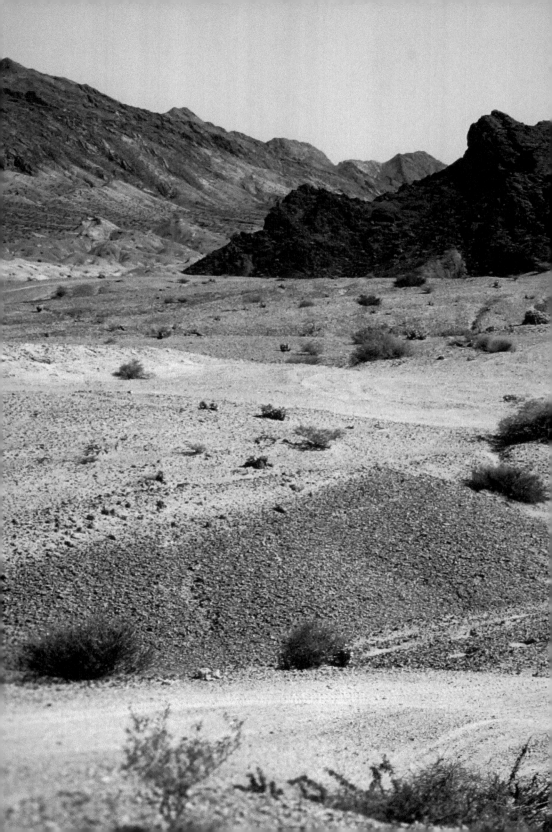

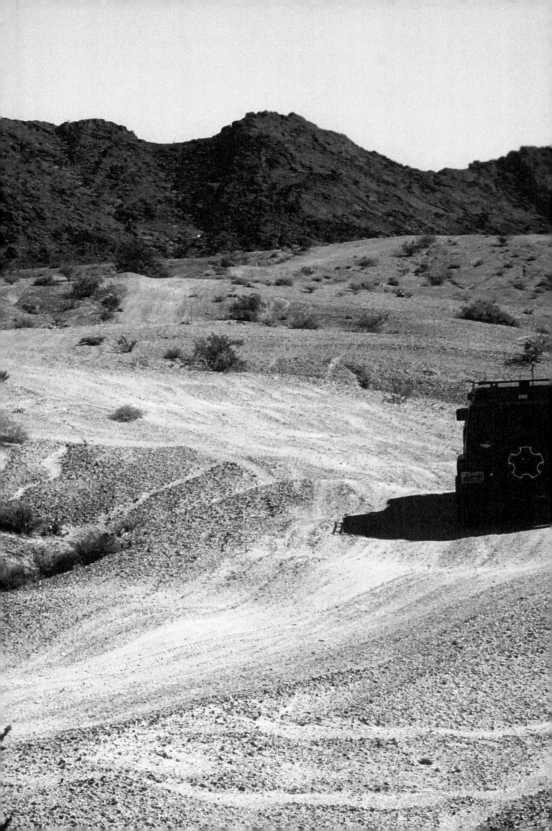

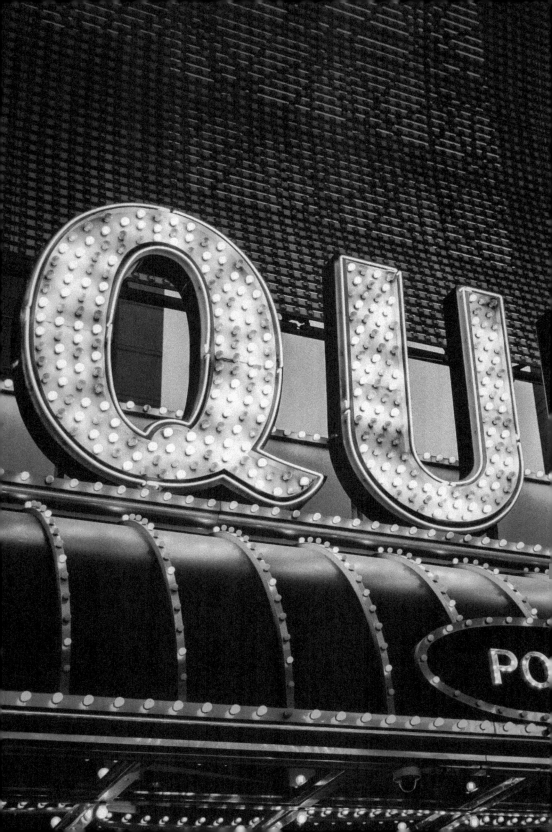

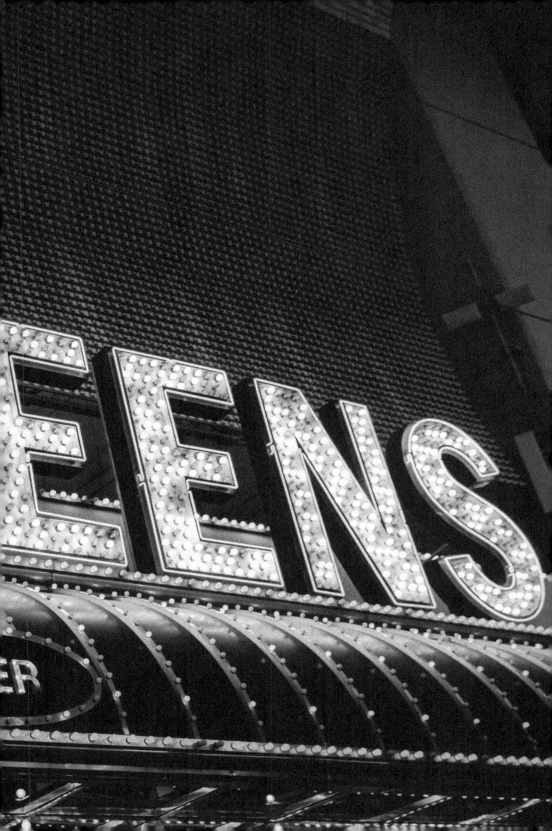

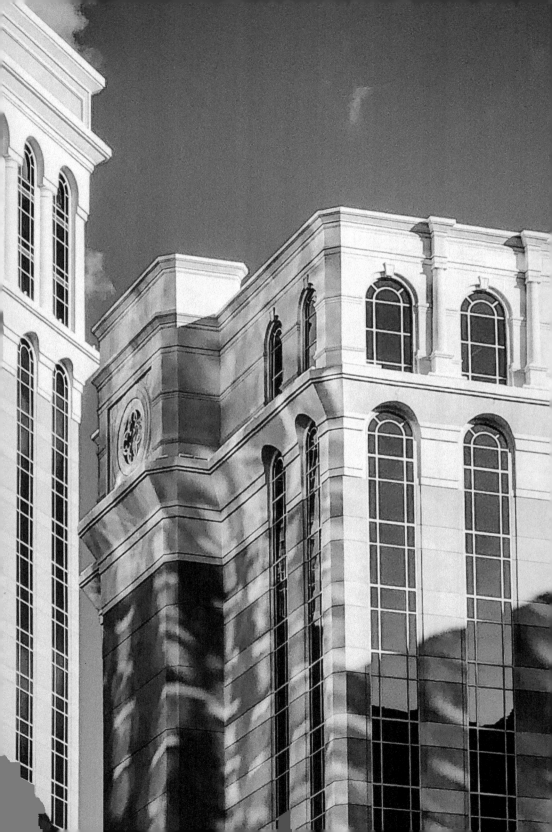

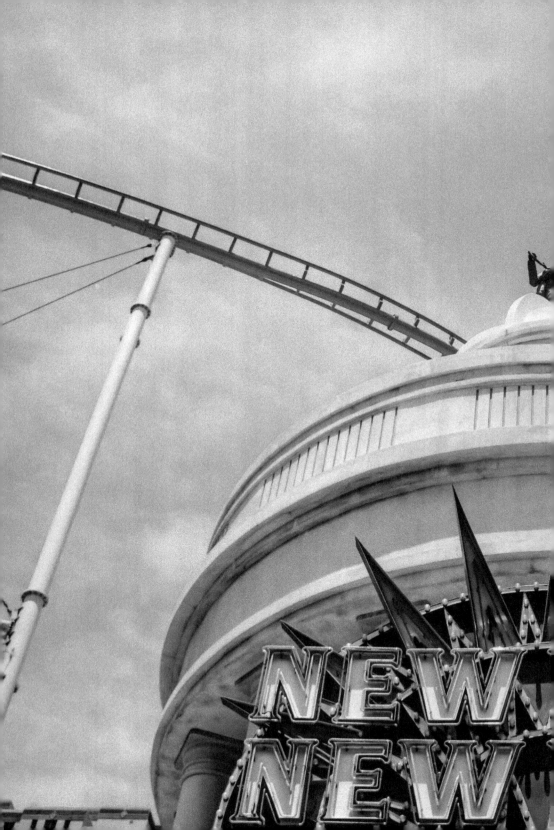

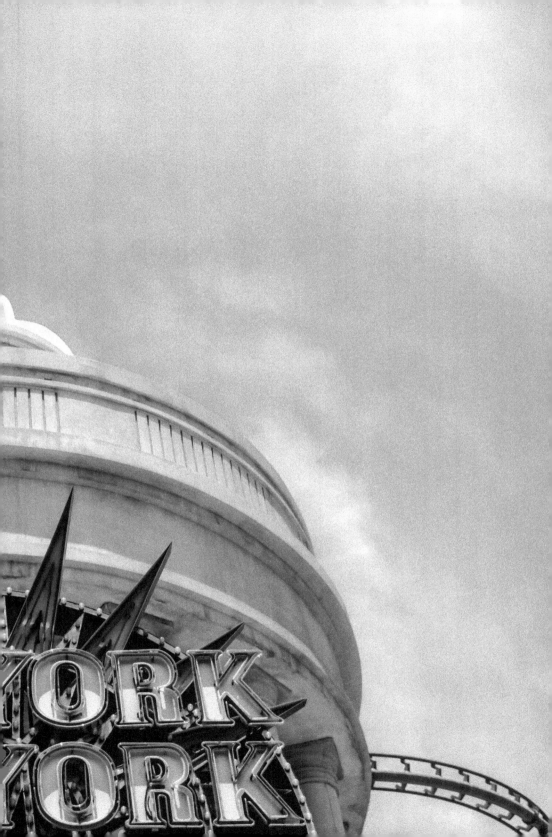

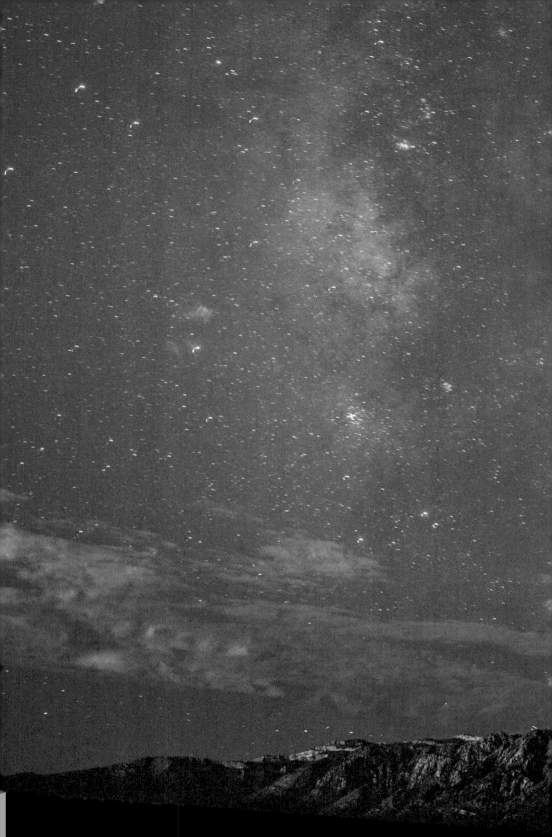

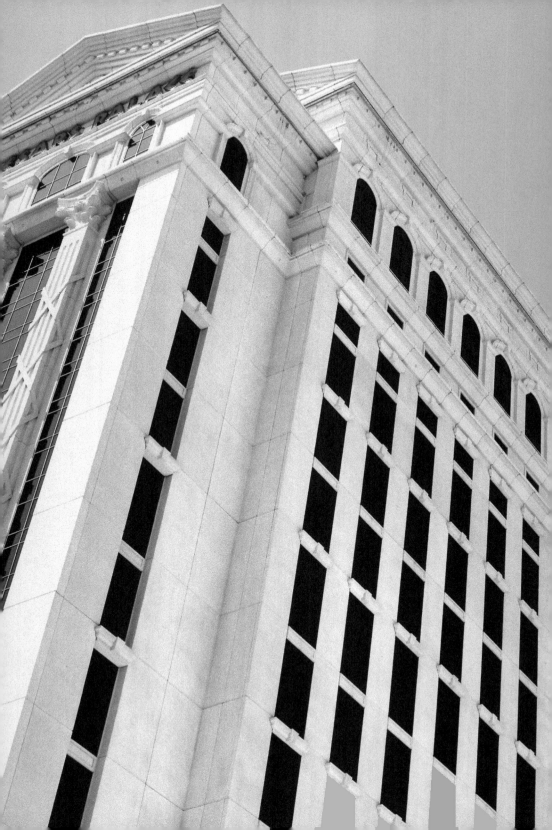

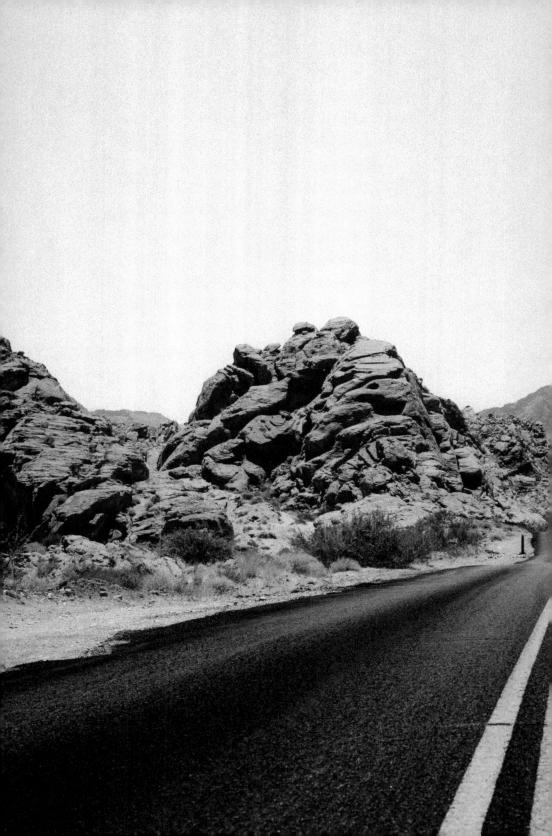

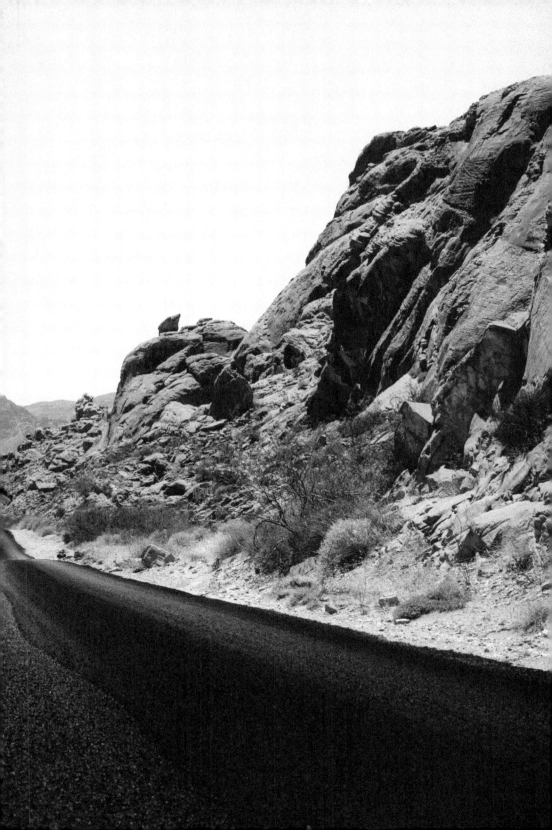

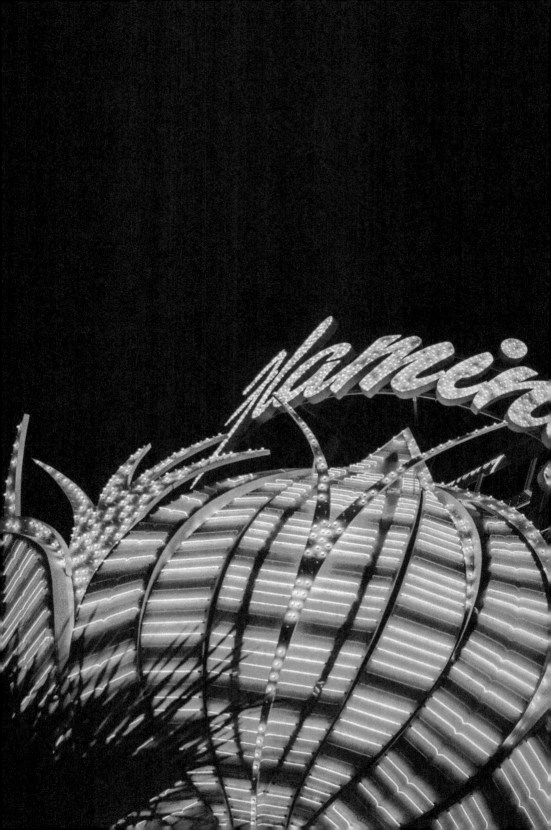

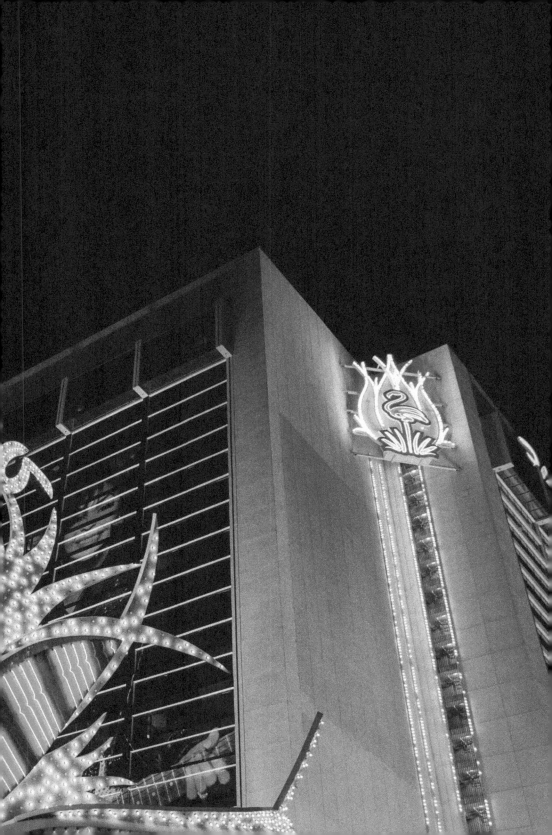

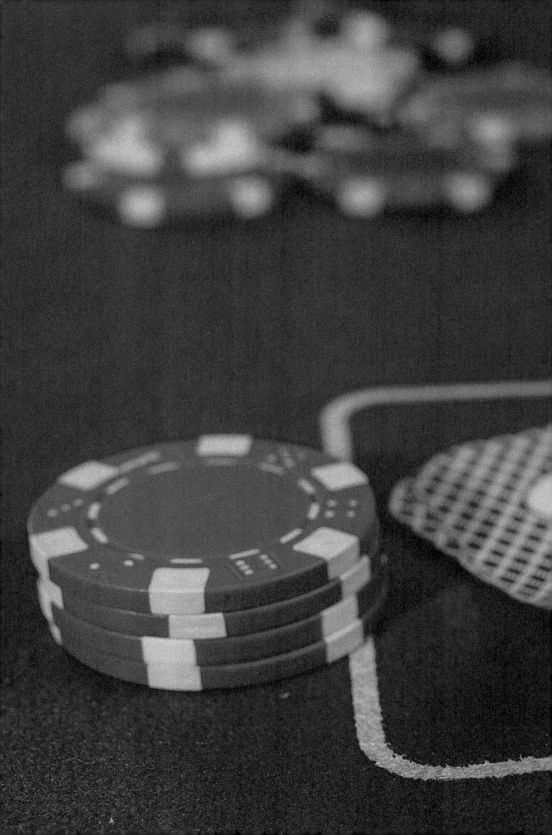

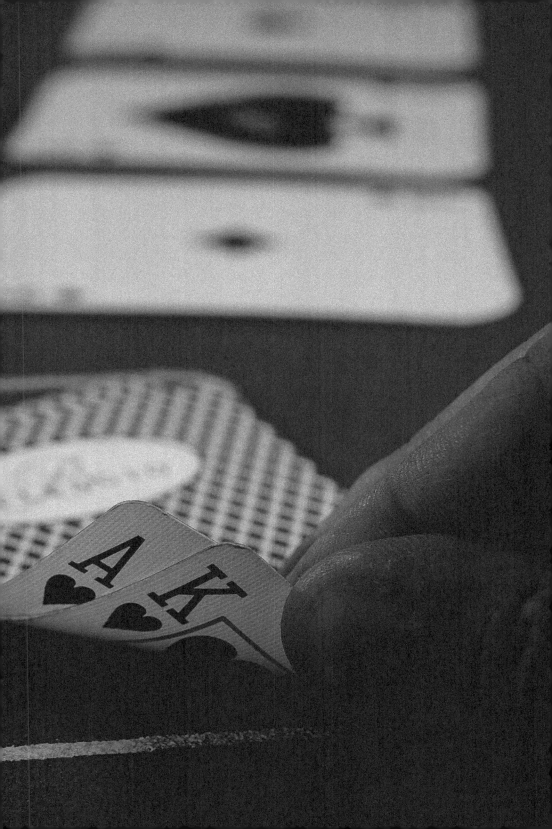

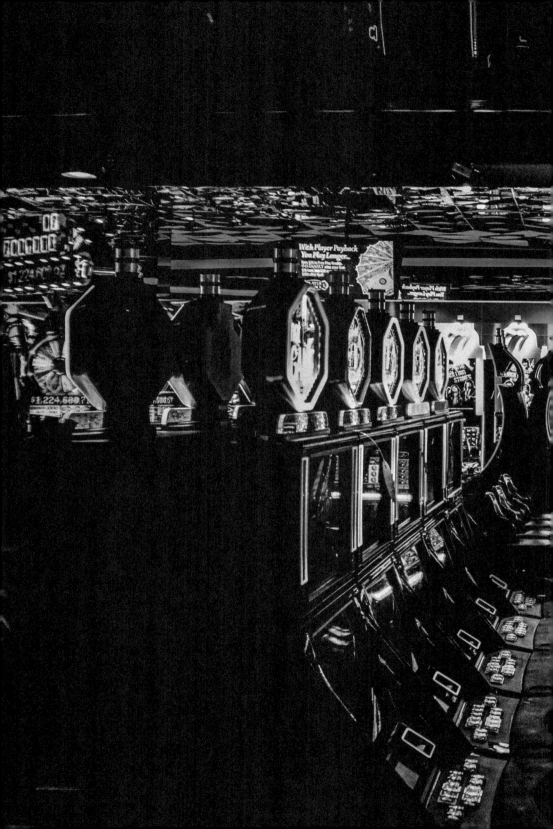

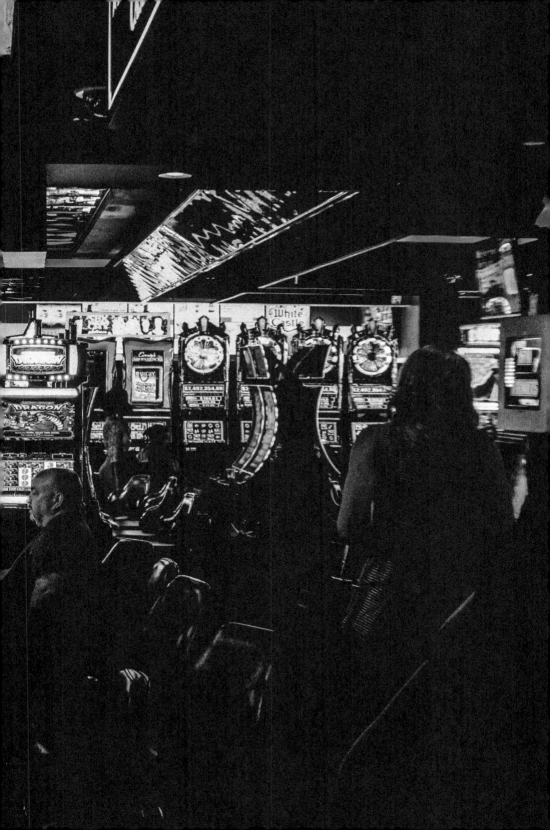

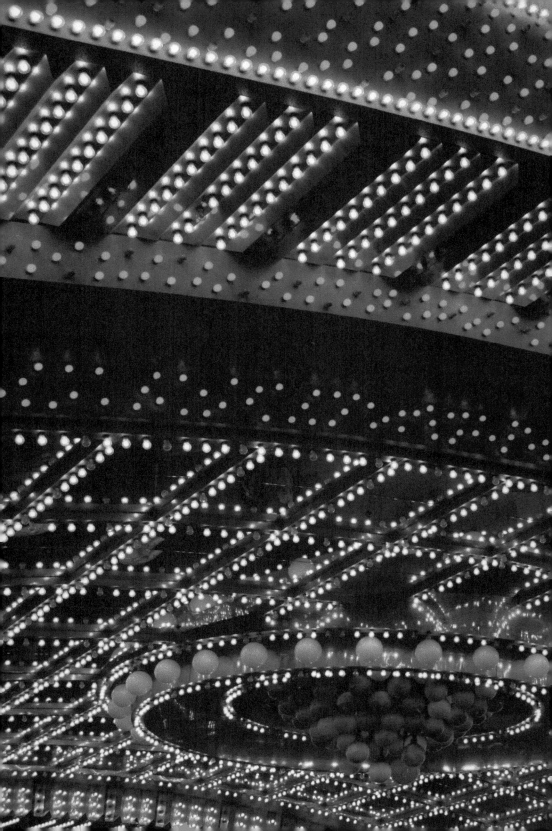

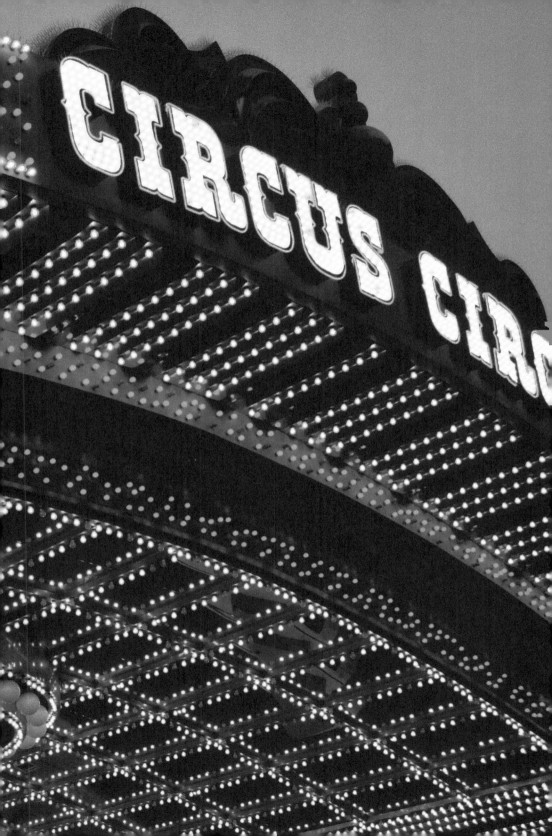

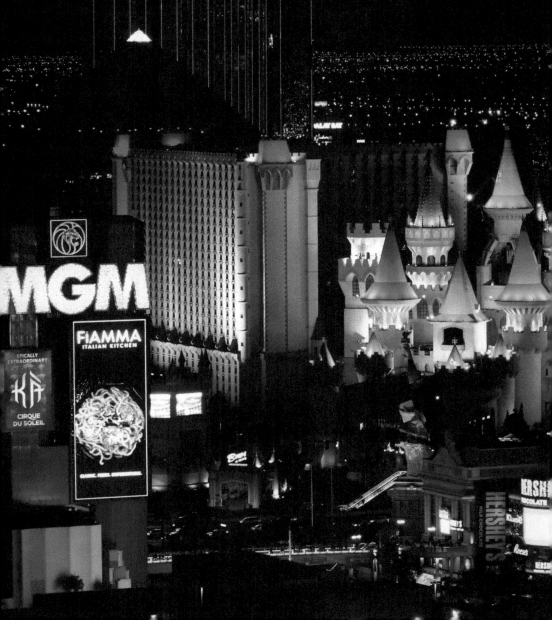

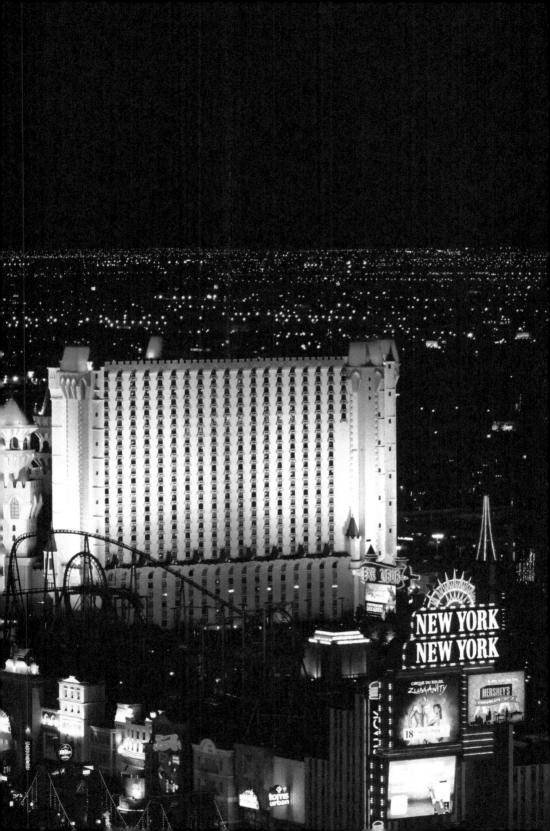

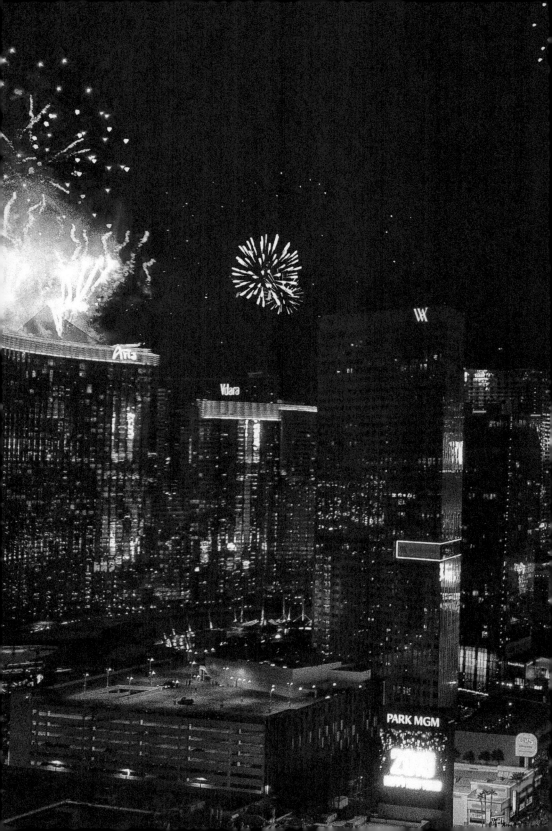

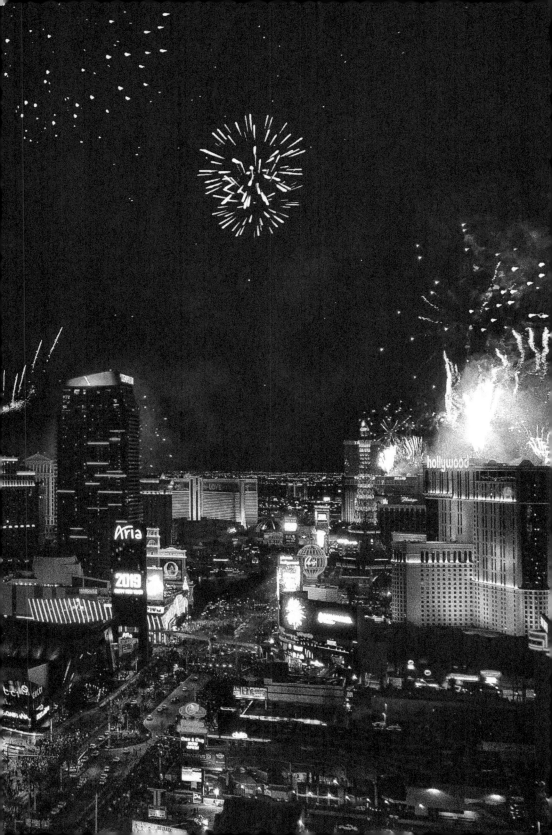

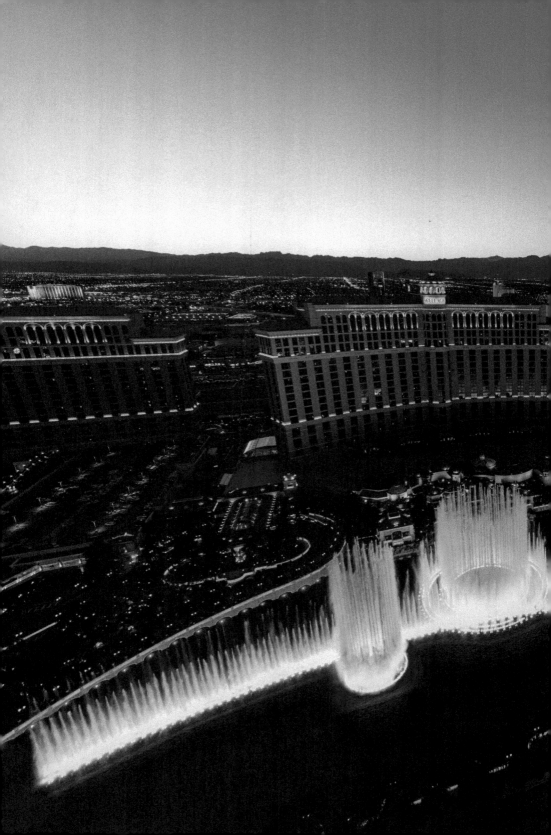

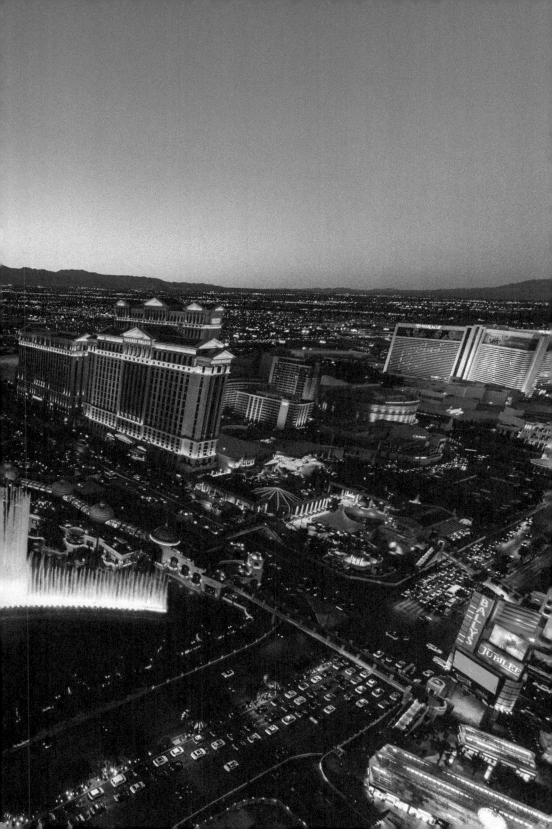

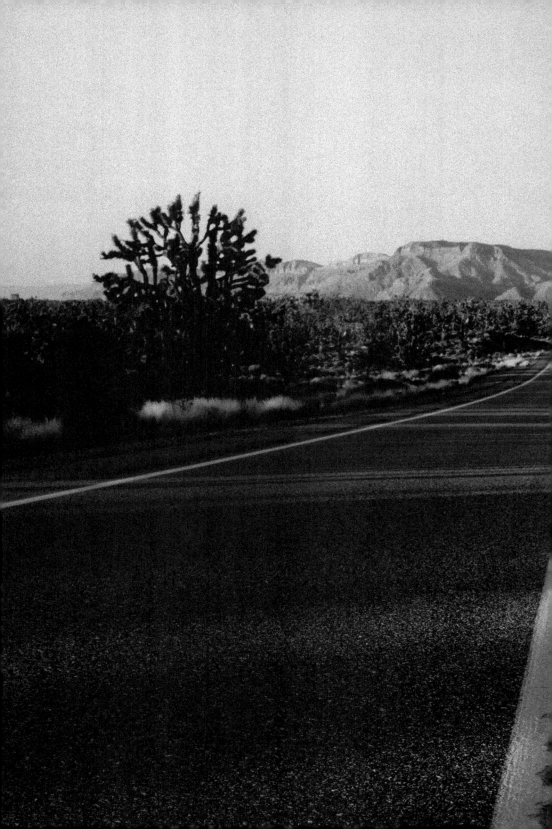

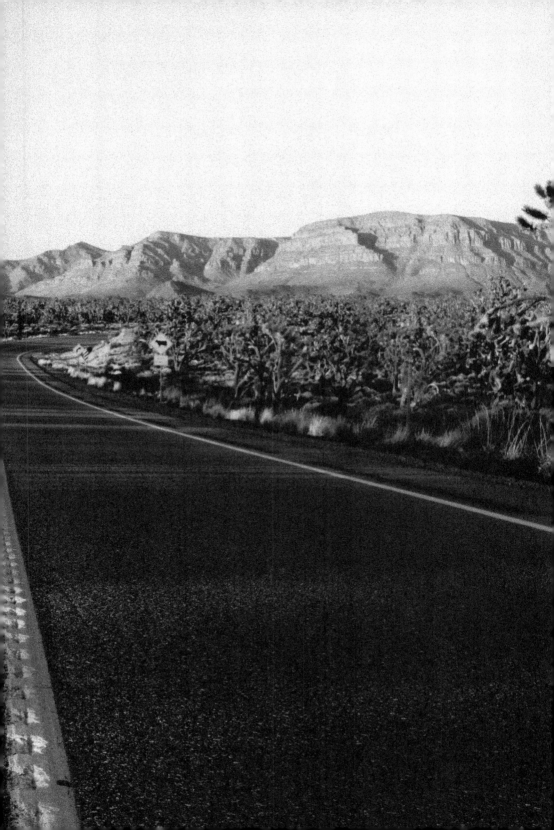

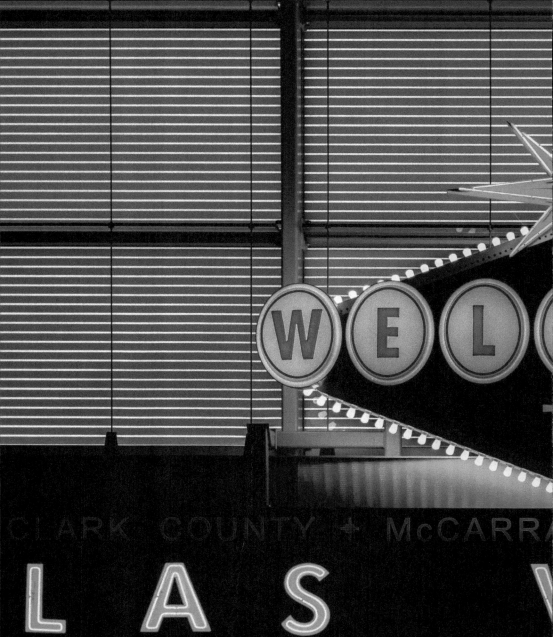

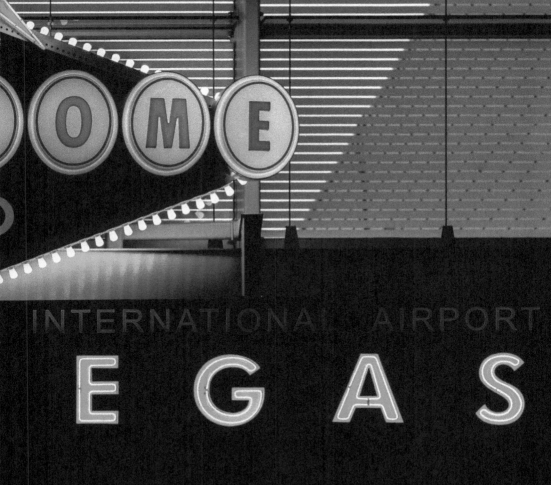

INTERNATIONAL AIRPORT

EGAS

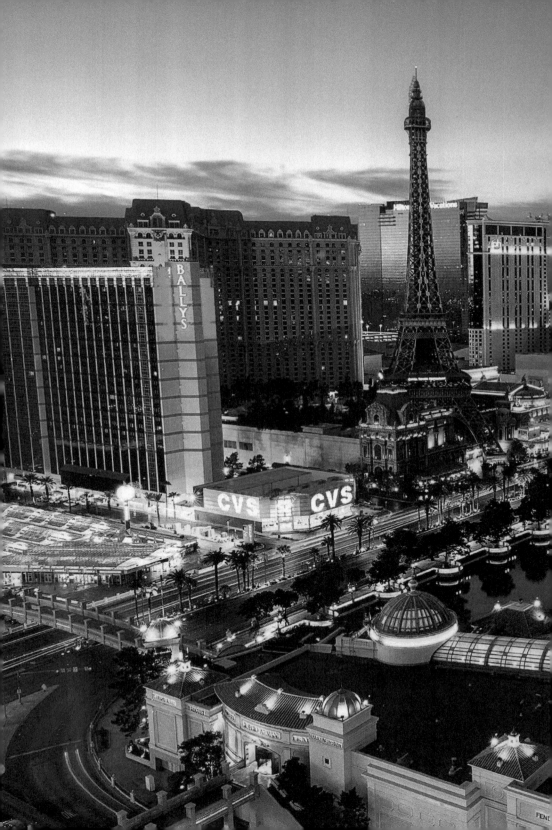

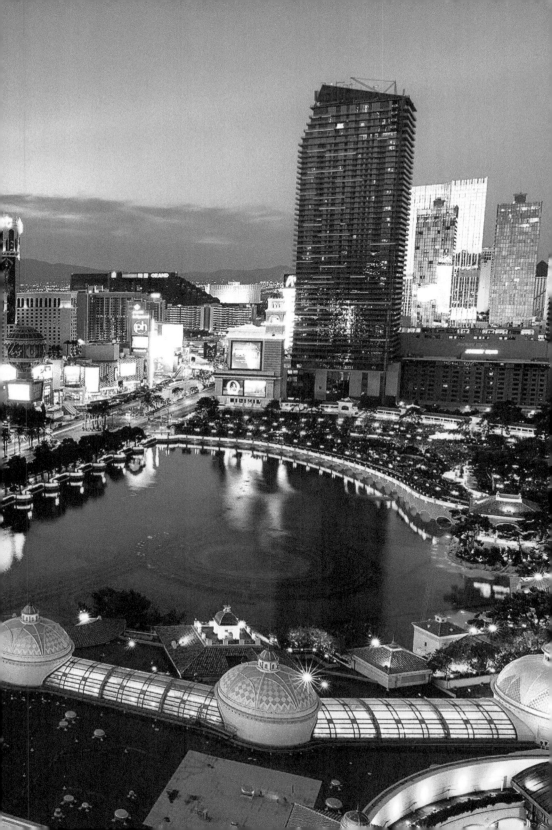

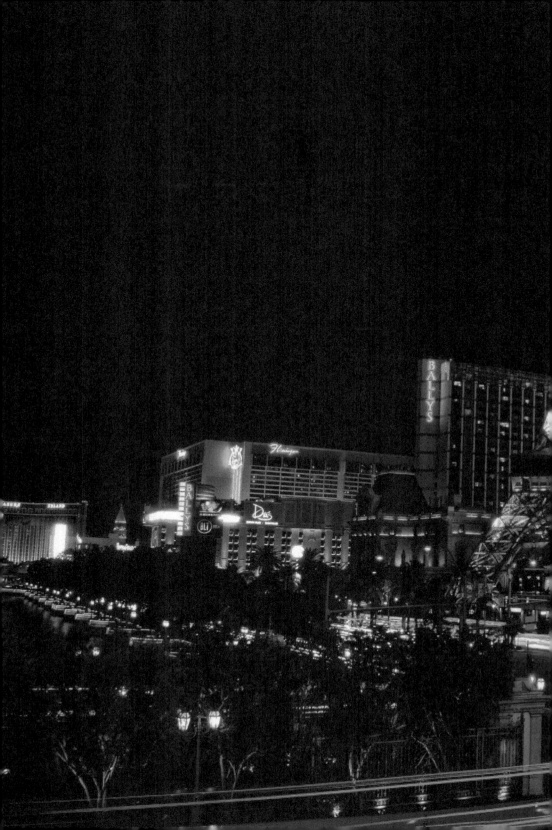

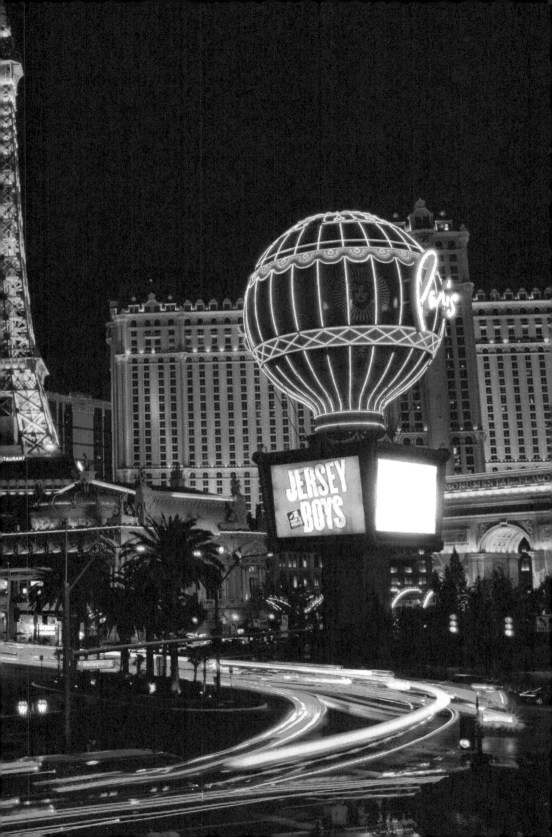

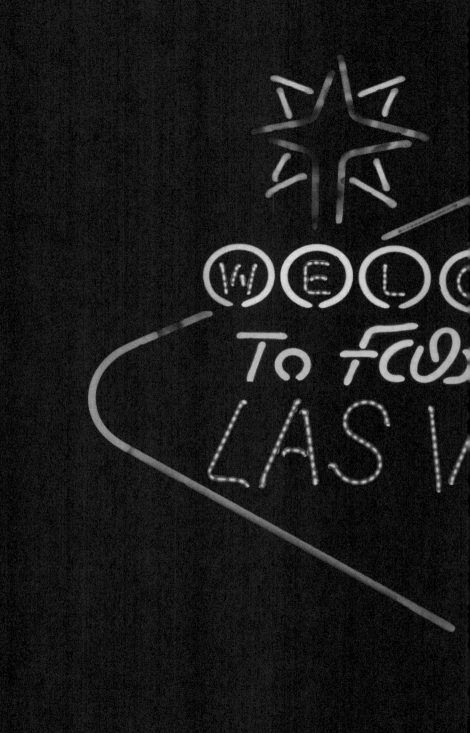

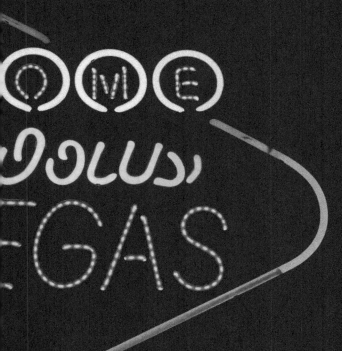

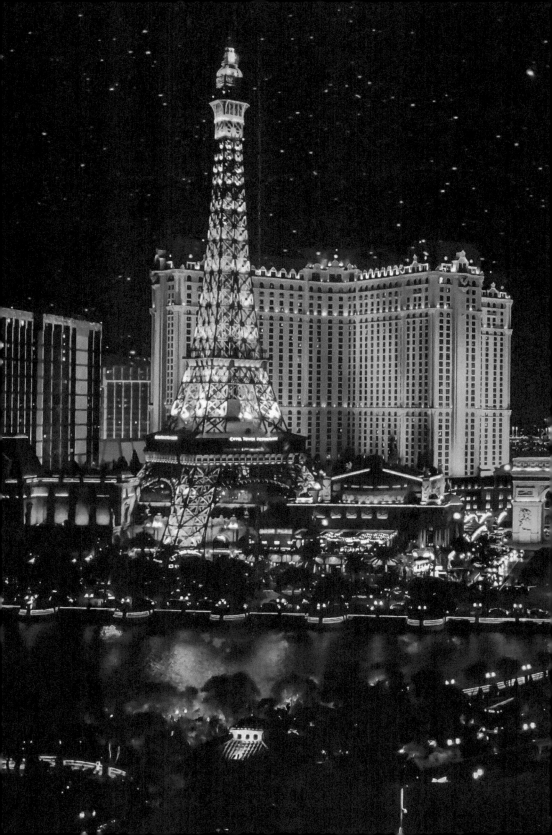

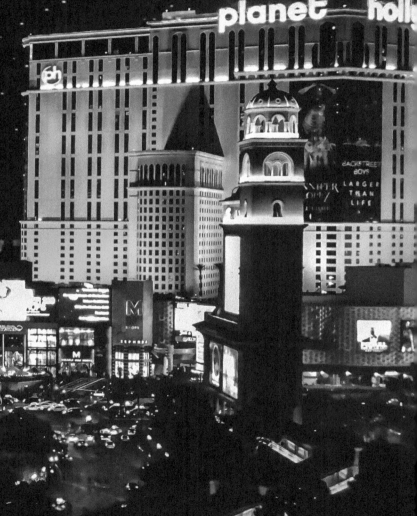

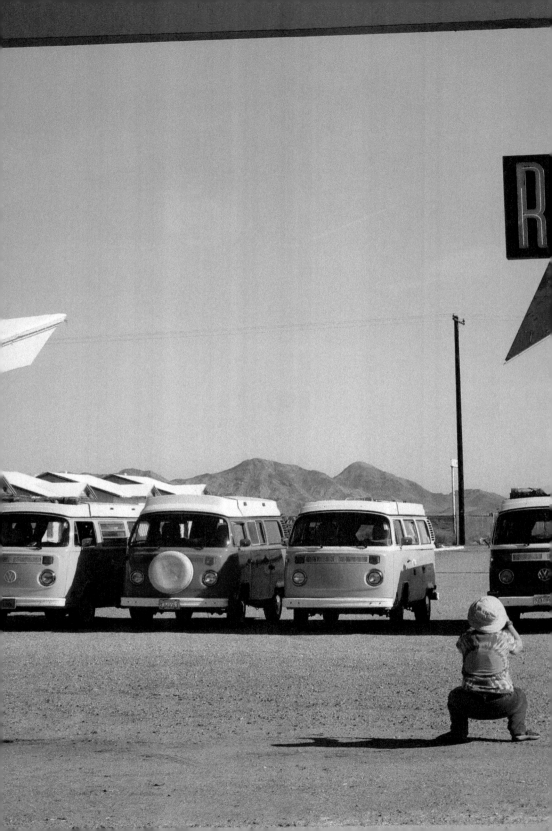

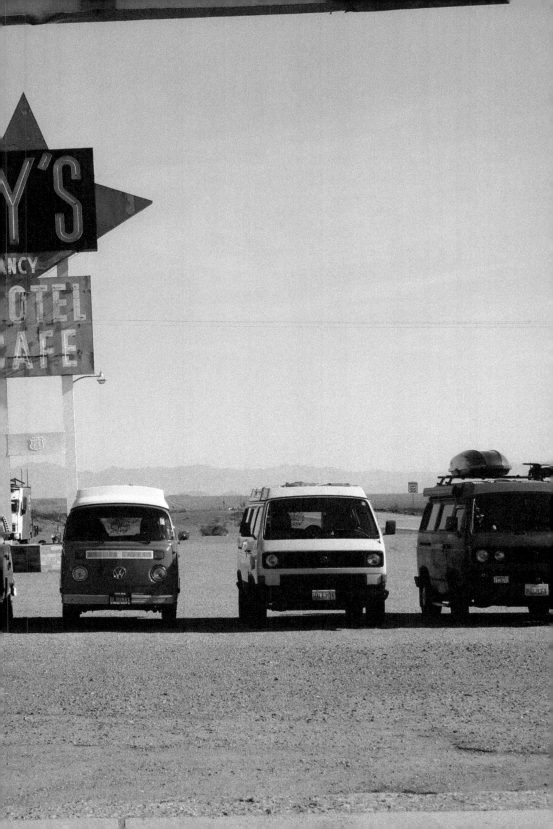

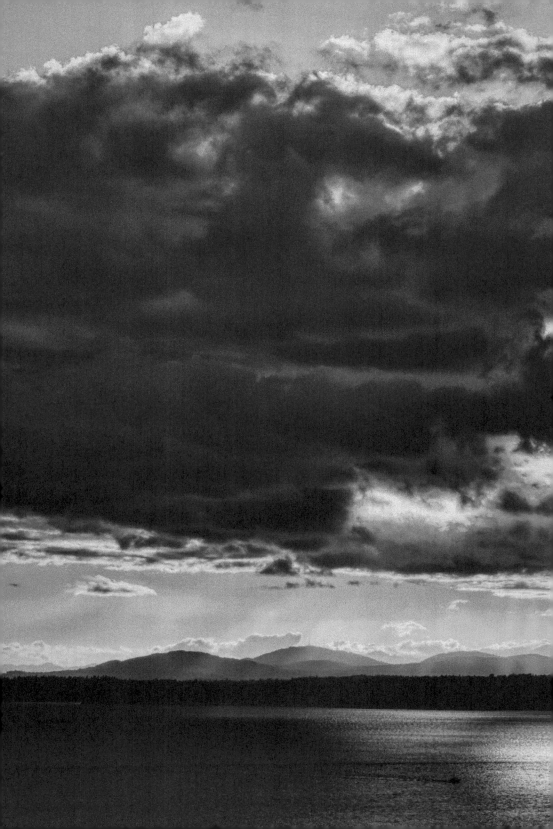

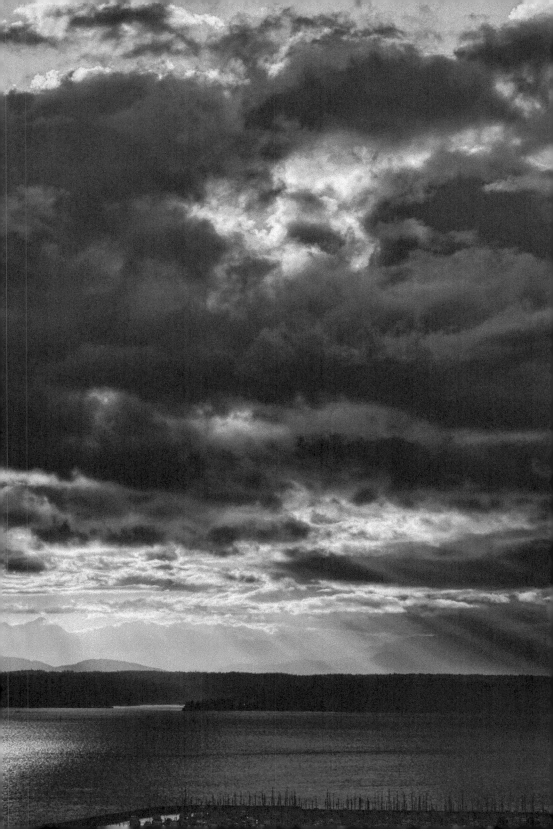

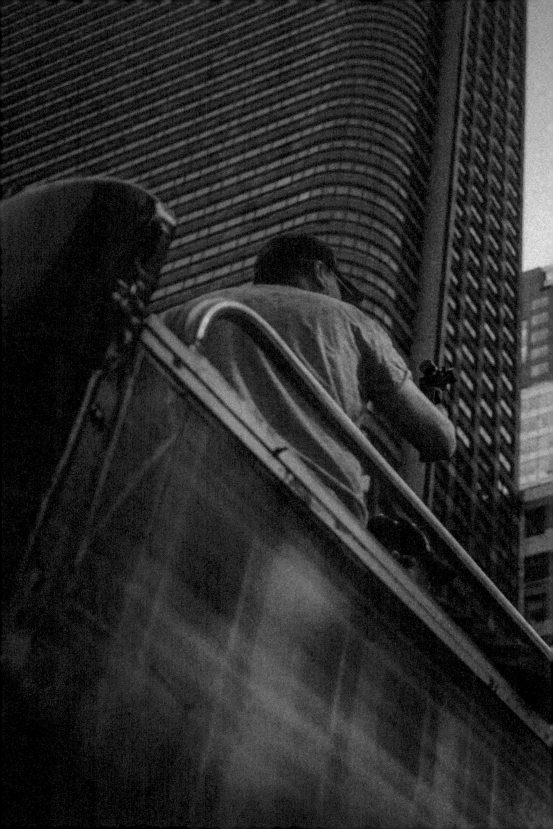

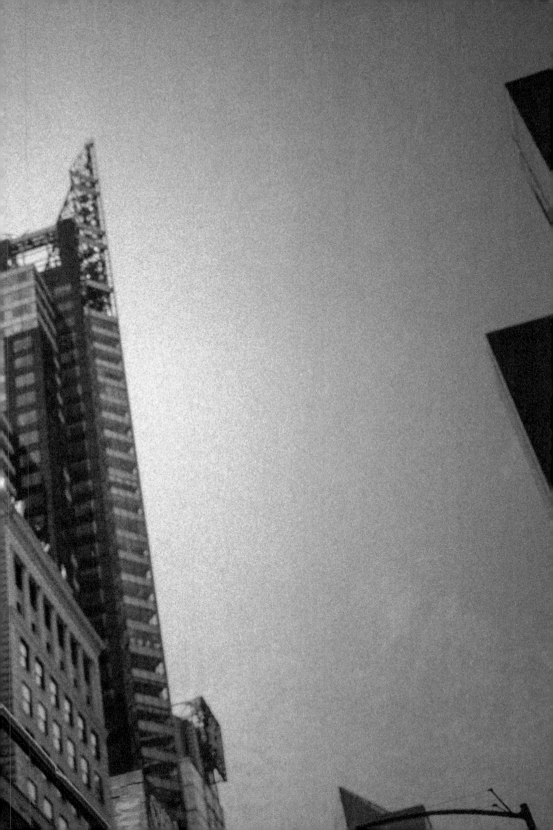

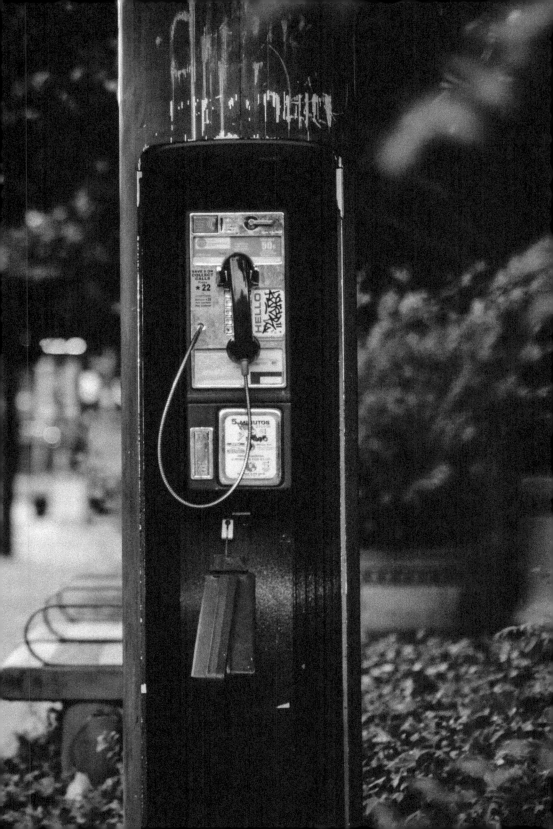

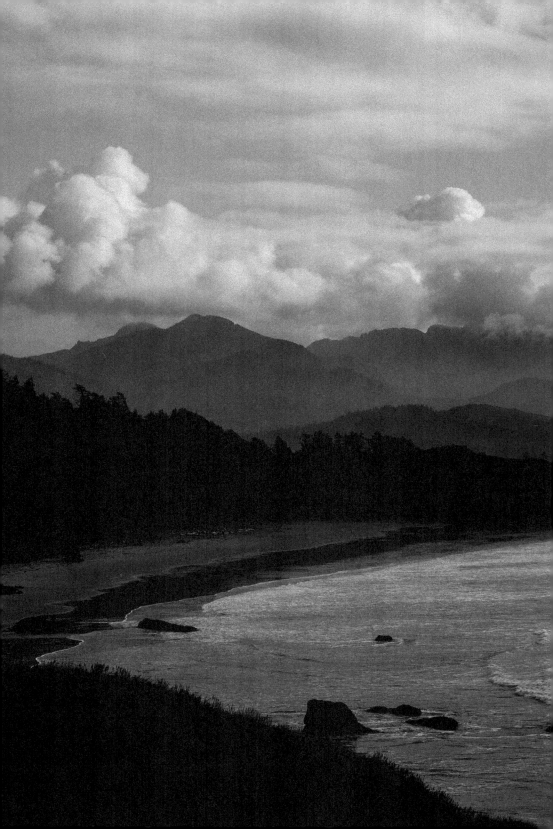

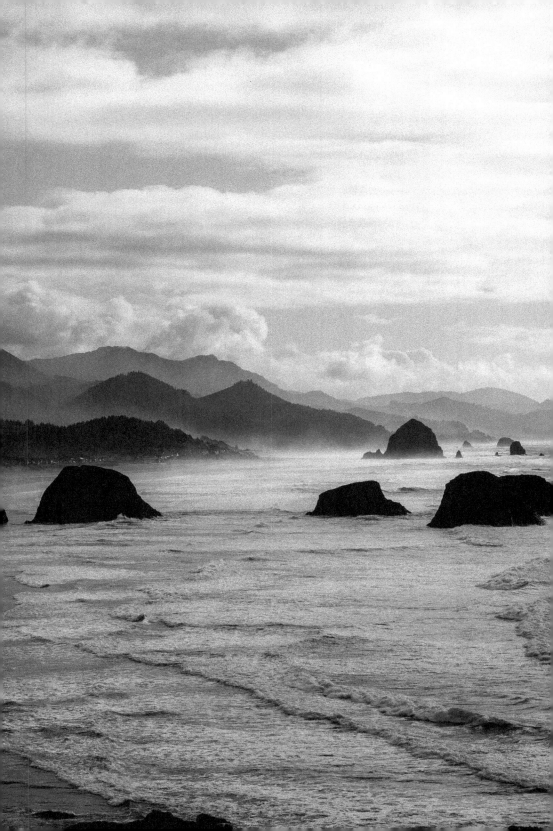

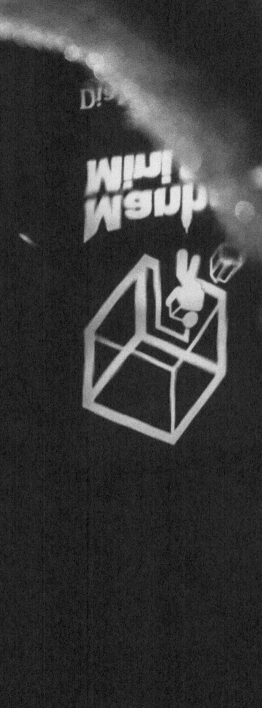

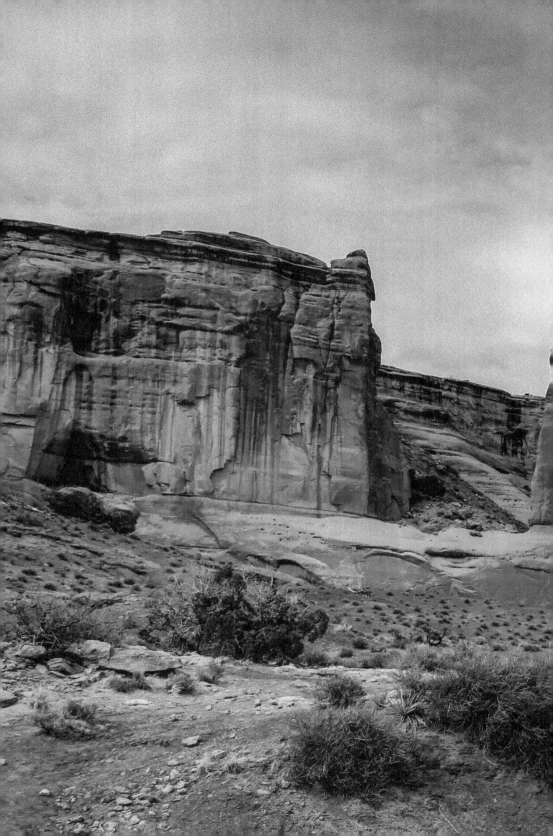

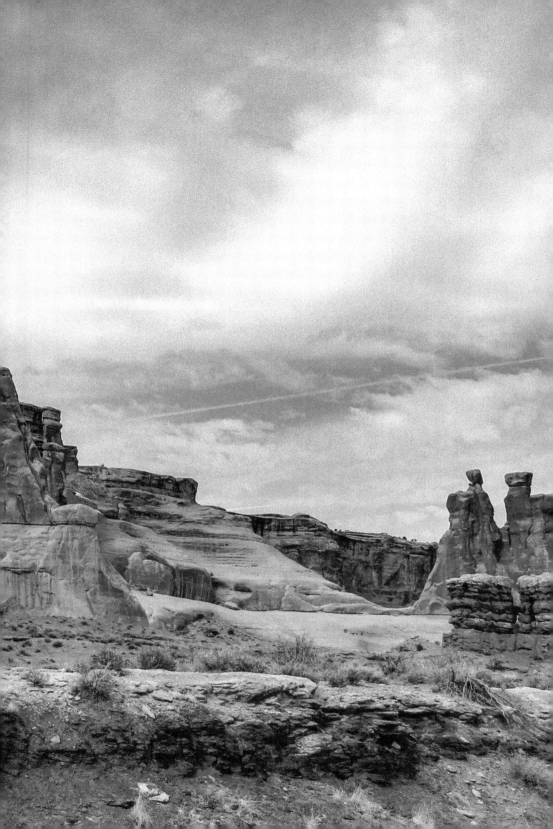

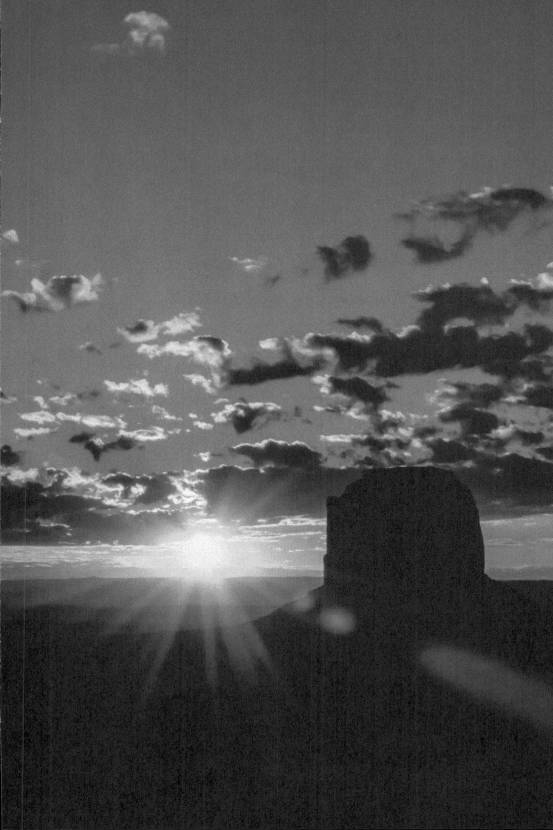

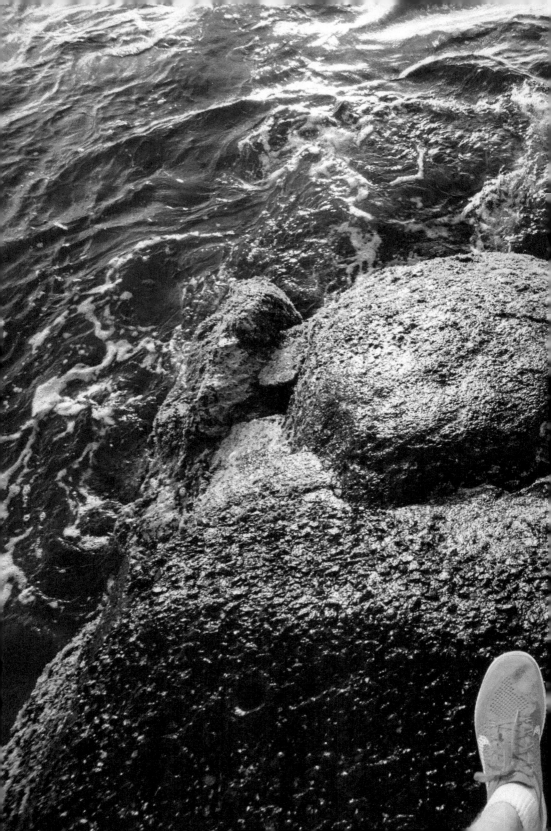

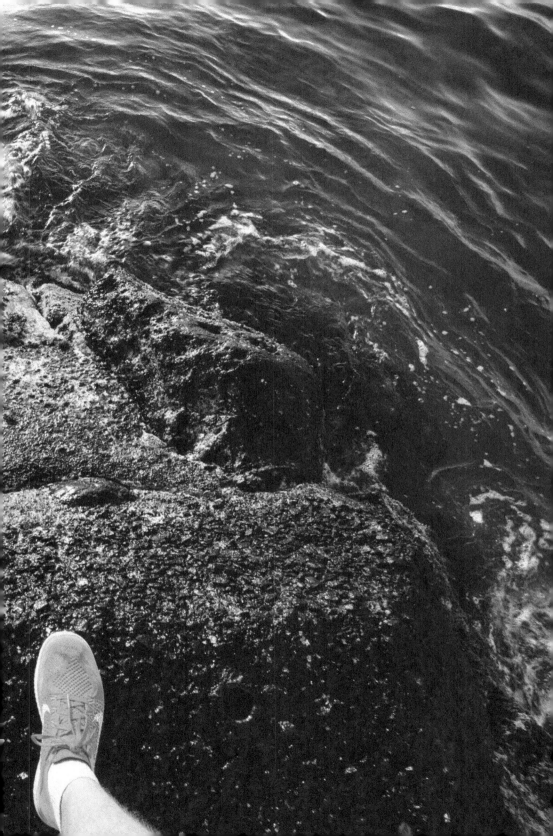

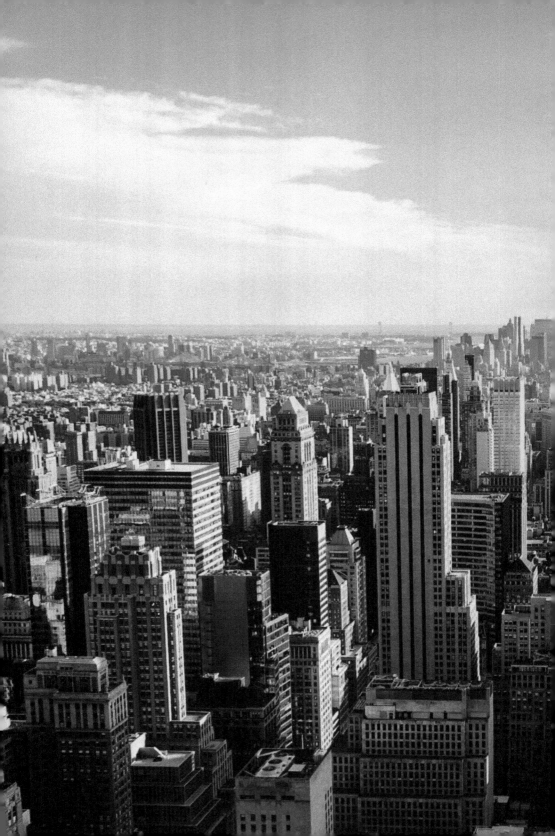

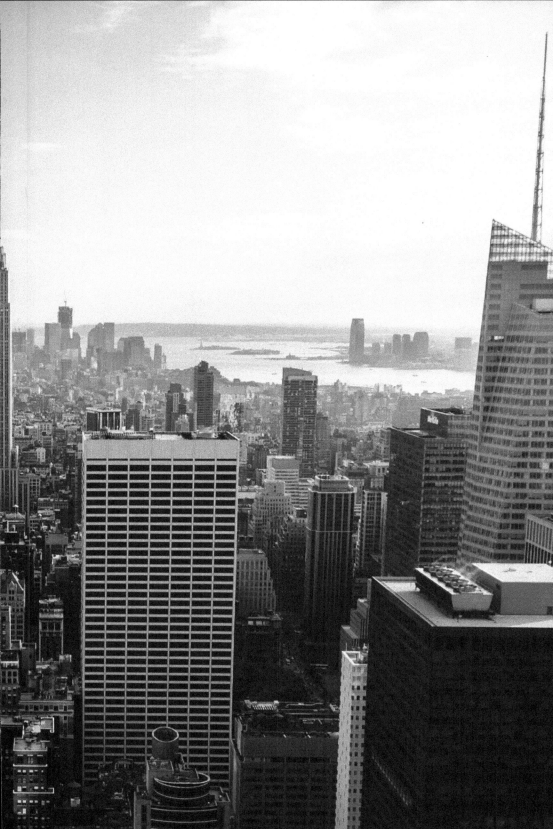

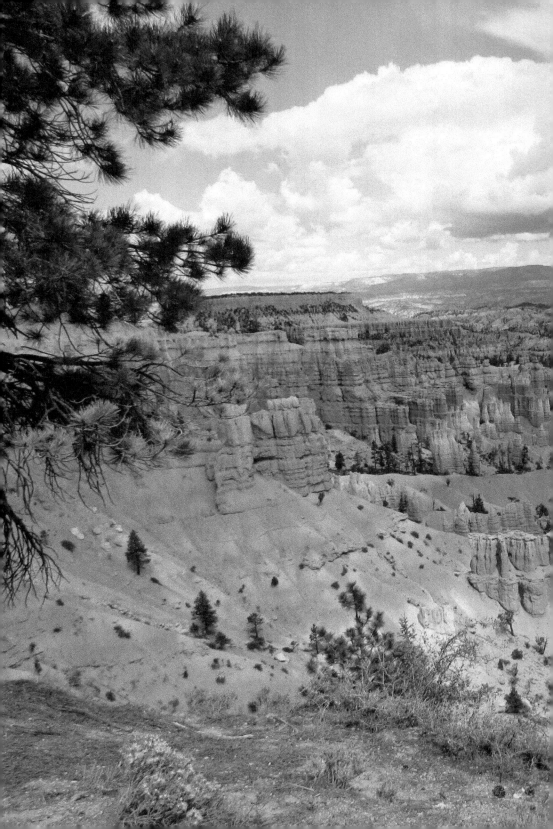

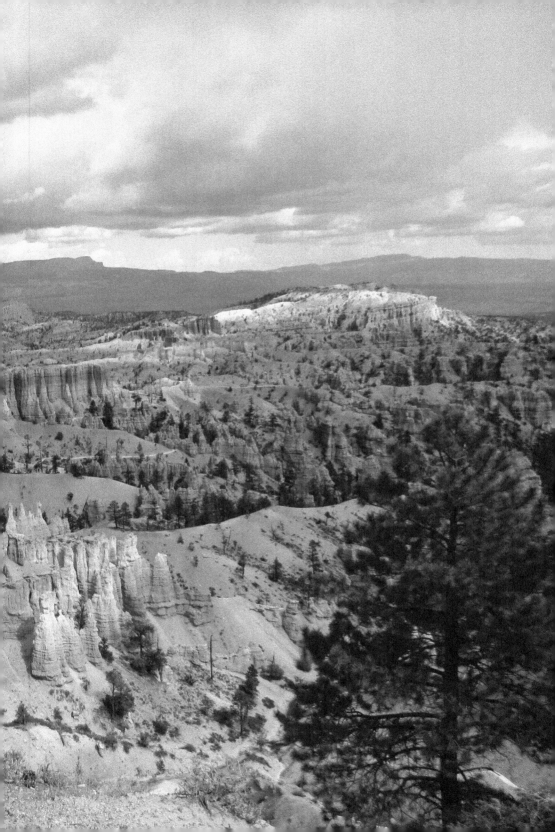

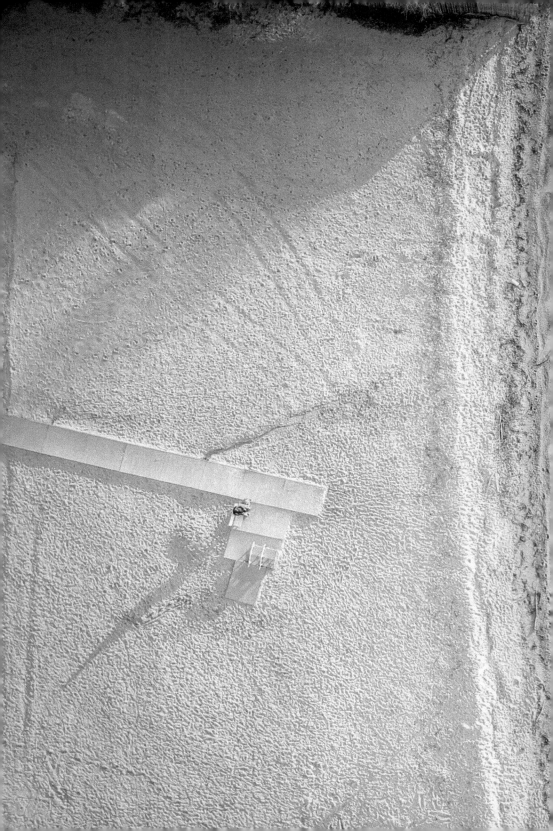

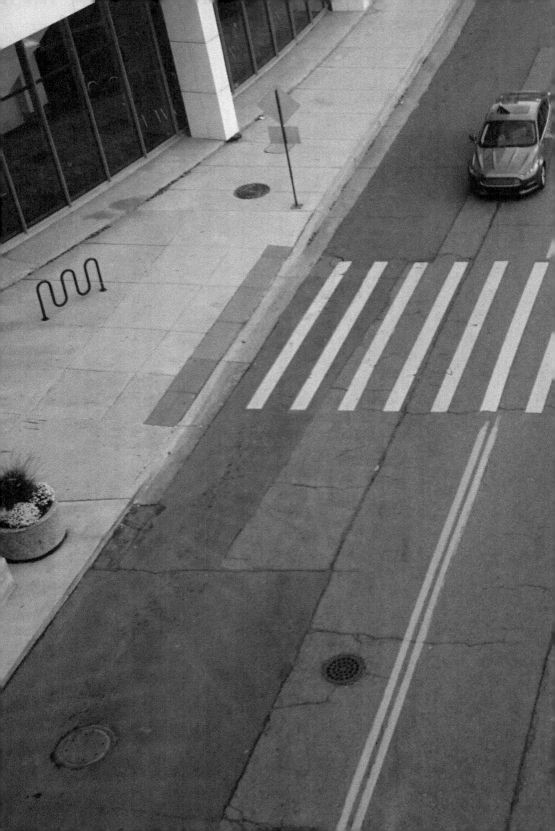

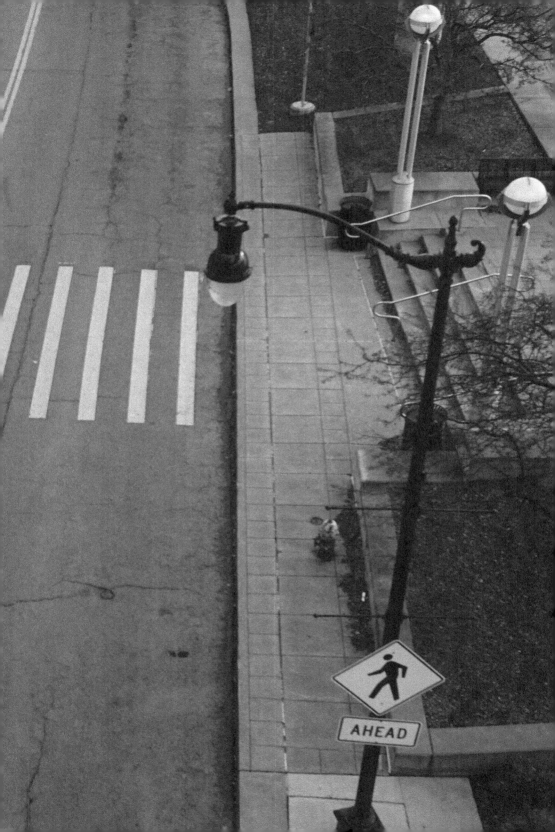

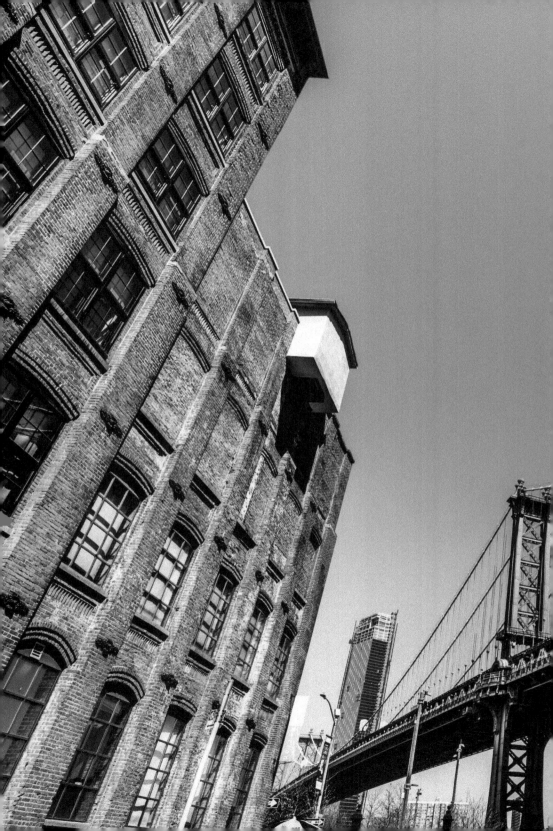

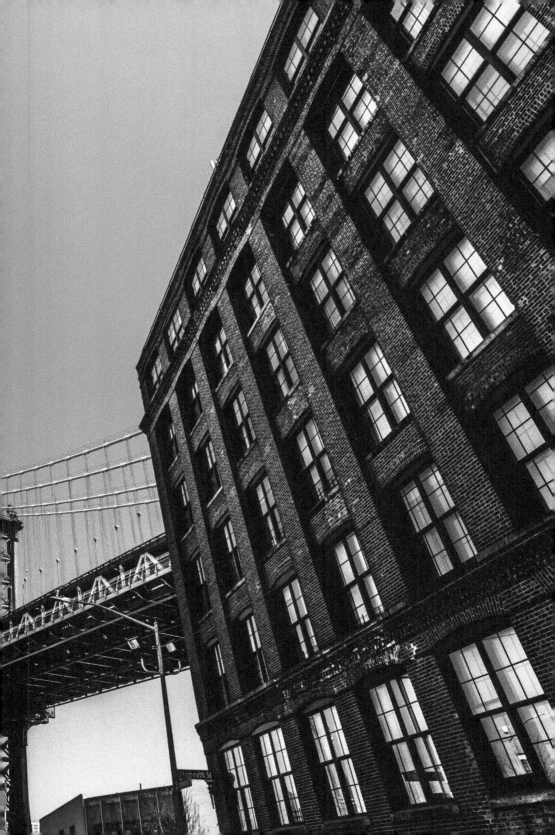

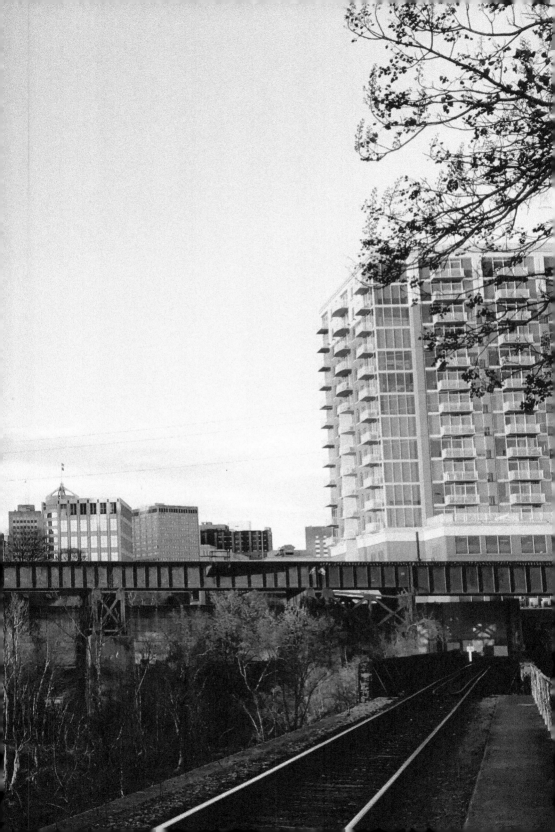

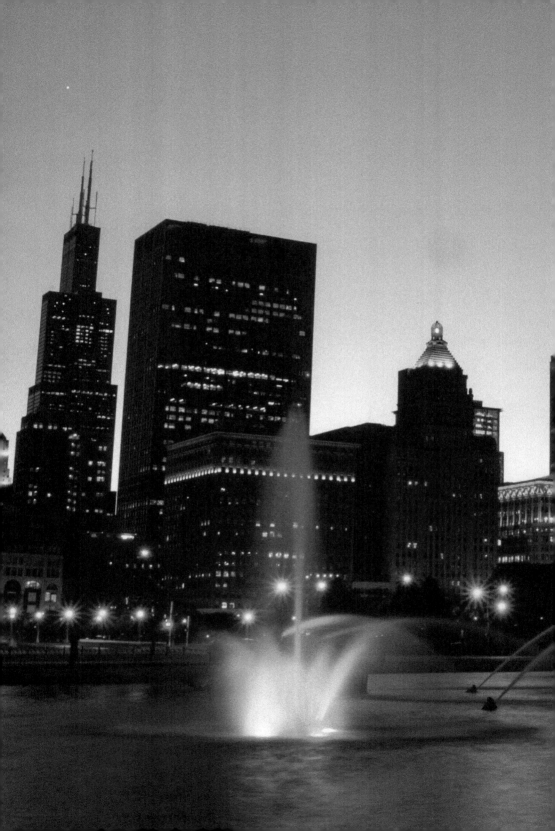

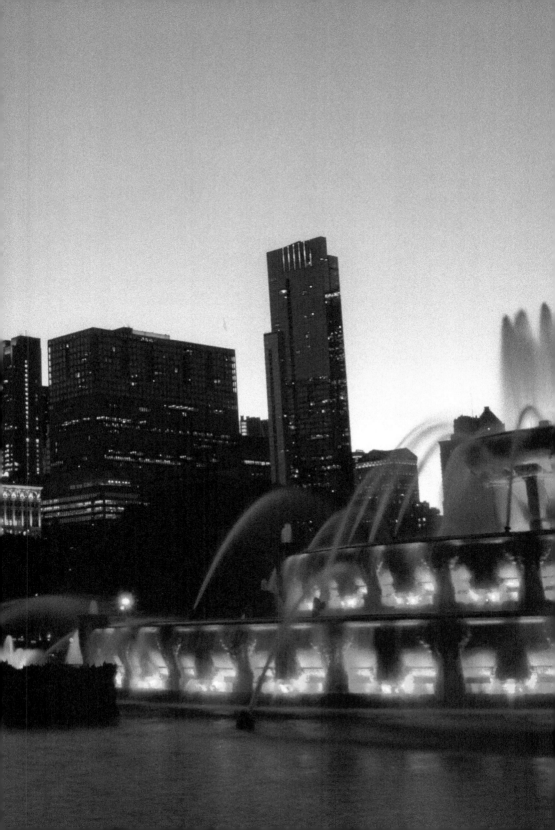

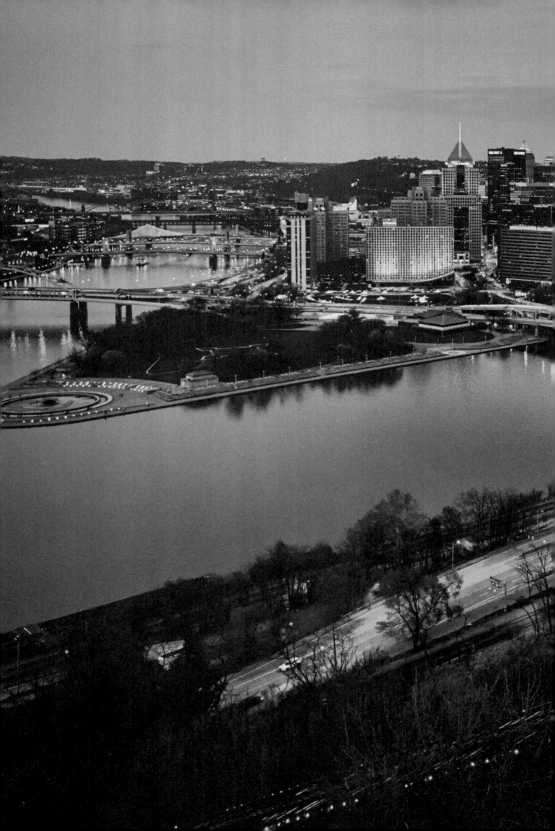

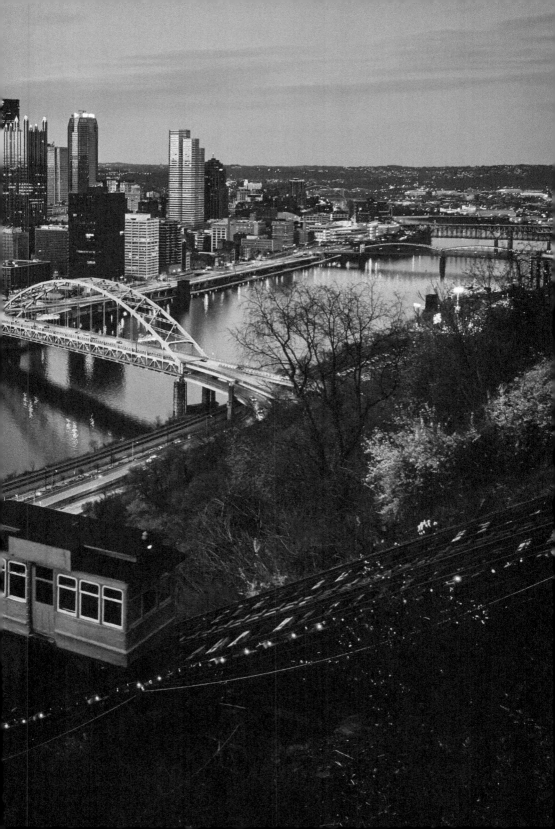

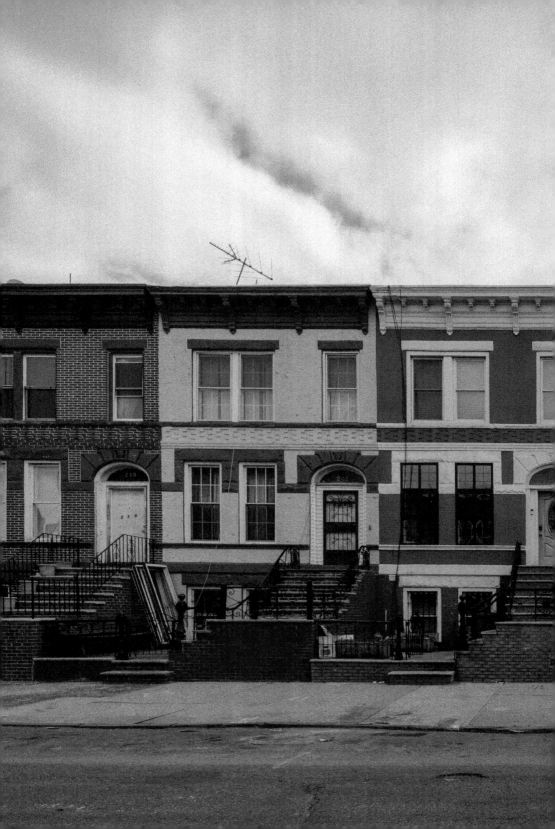

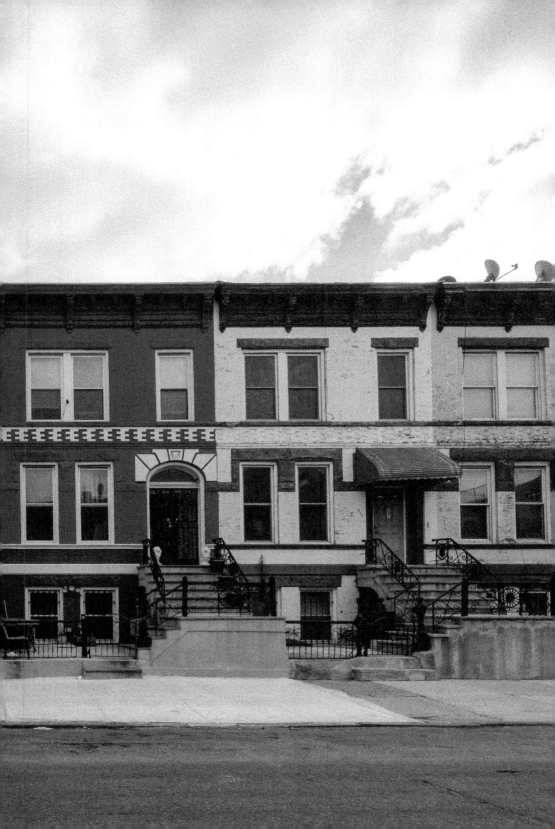

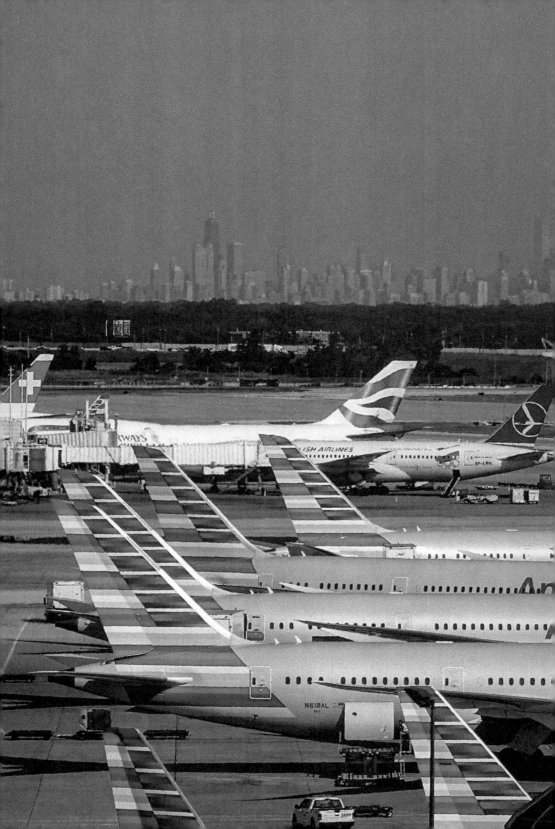

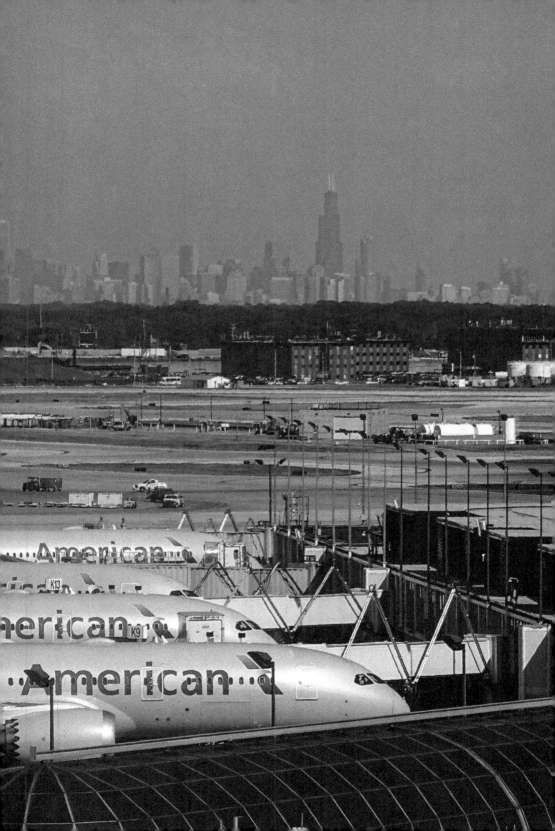

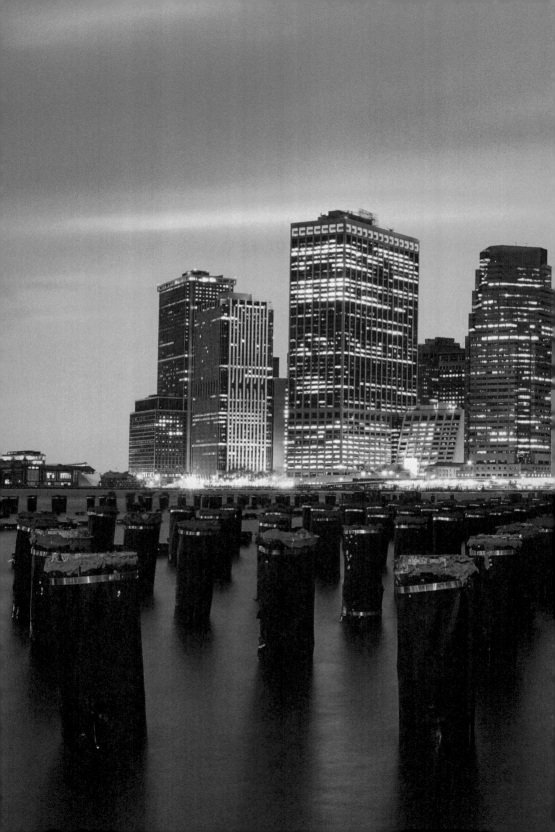

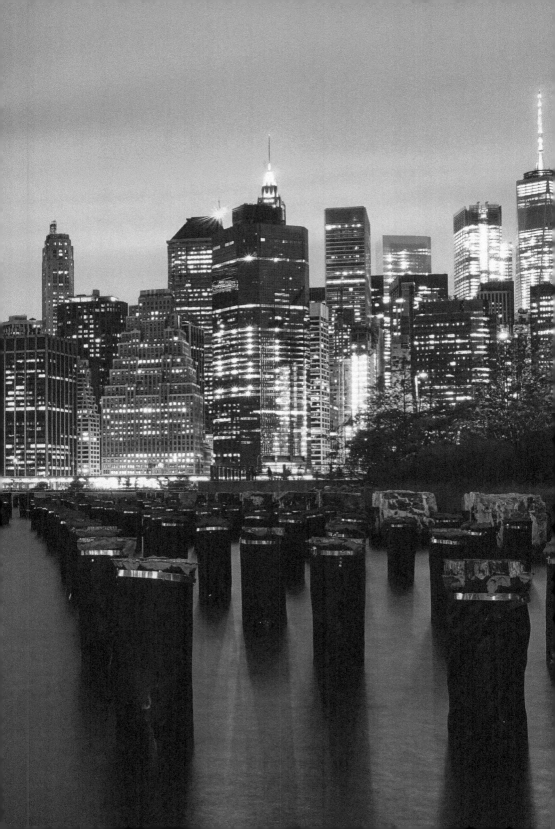

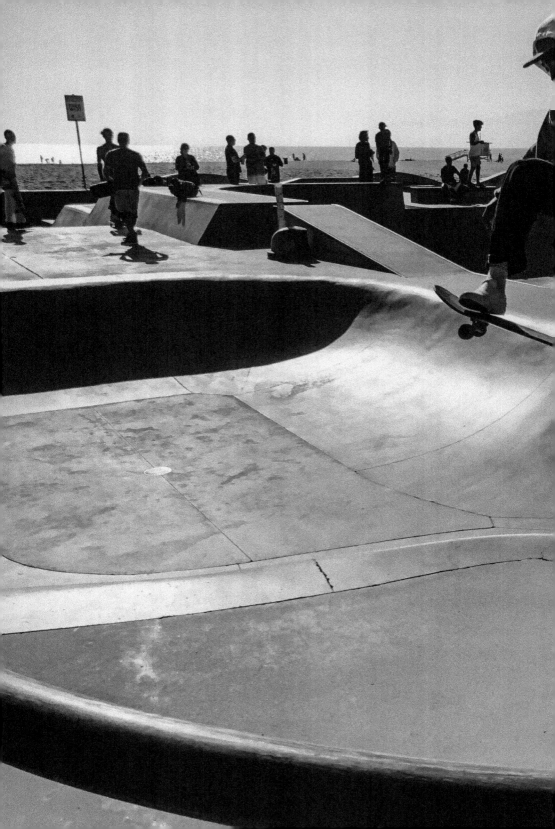

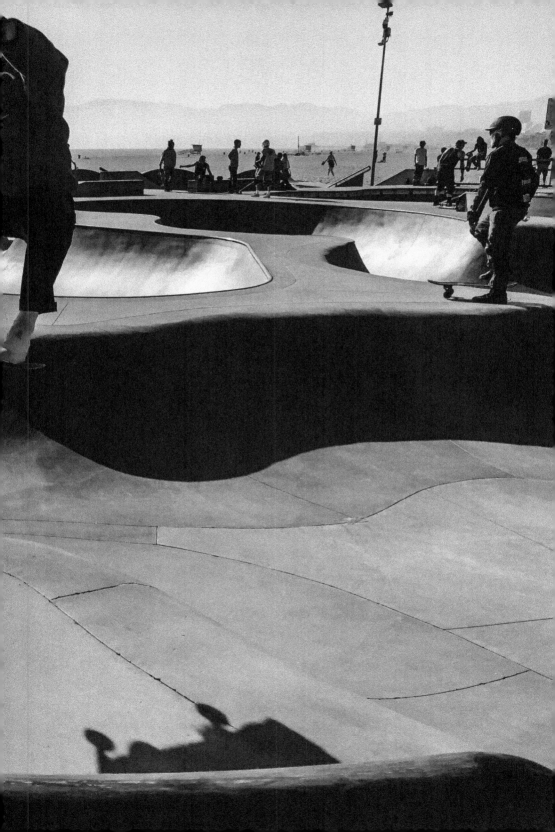

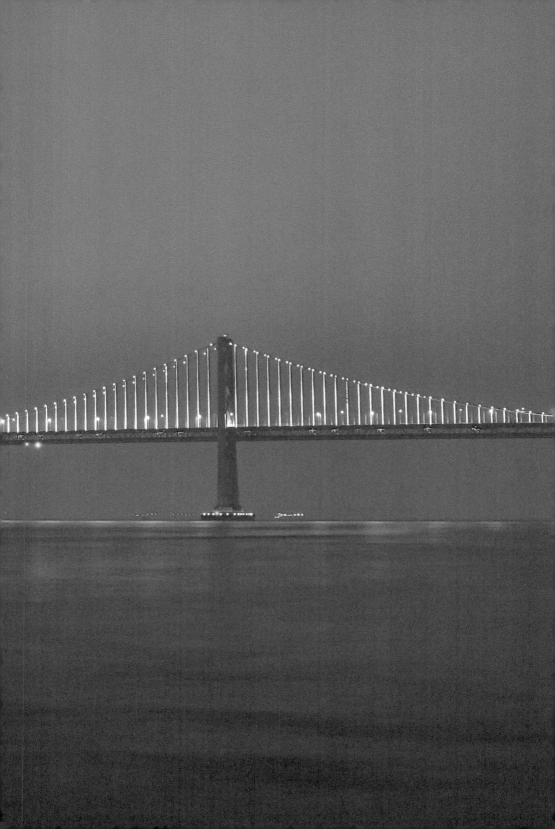

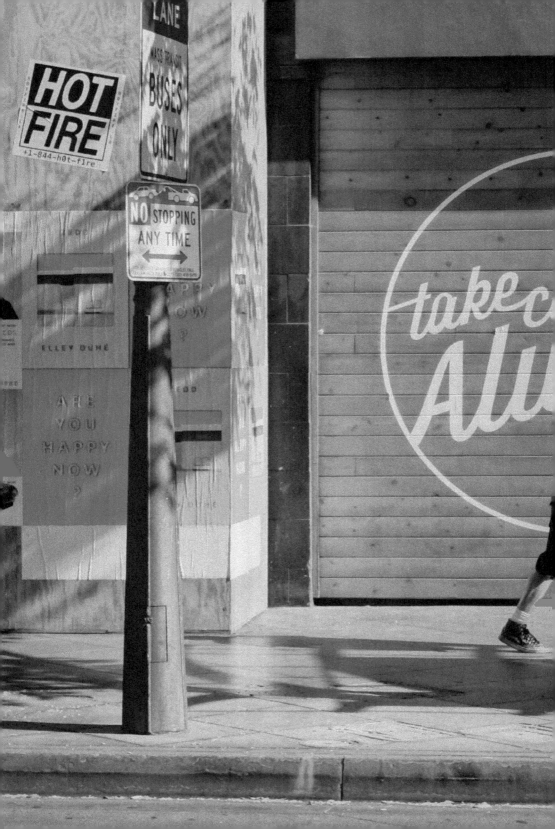

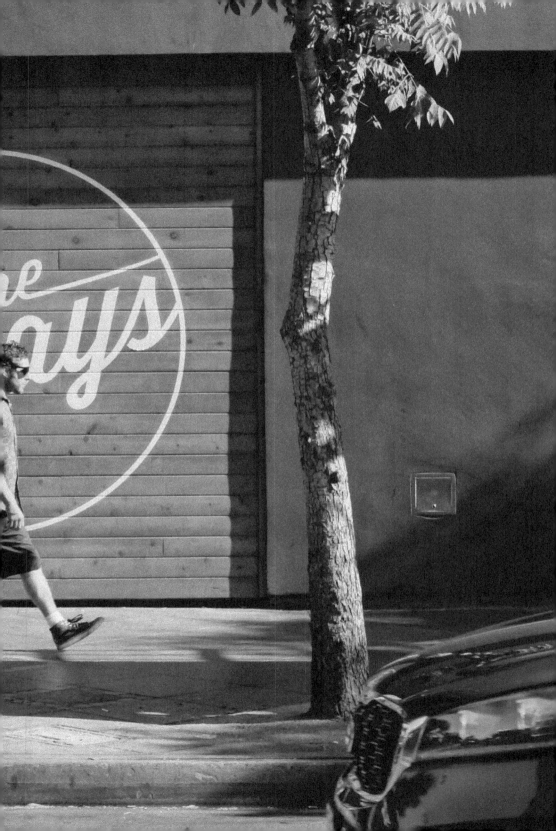

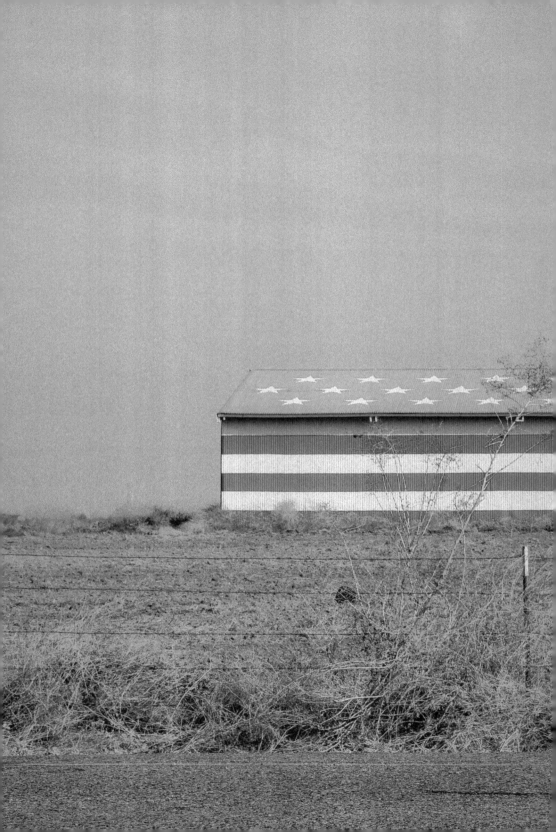

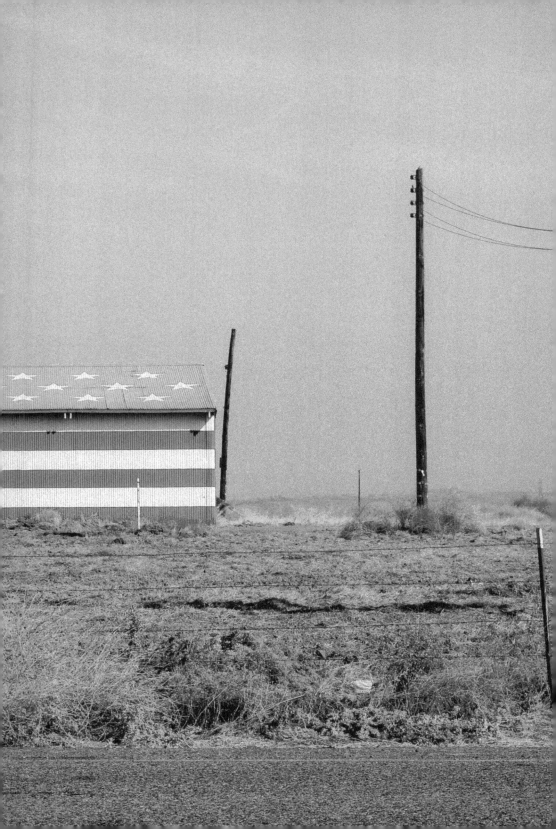

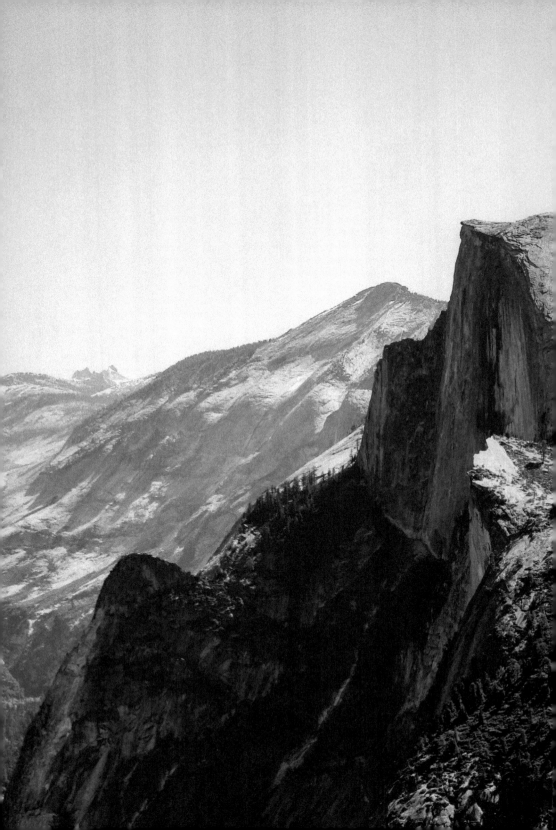

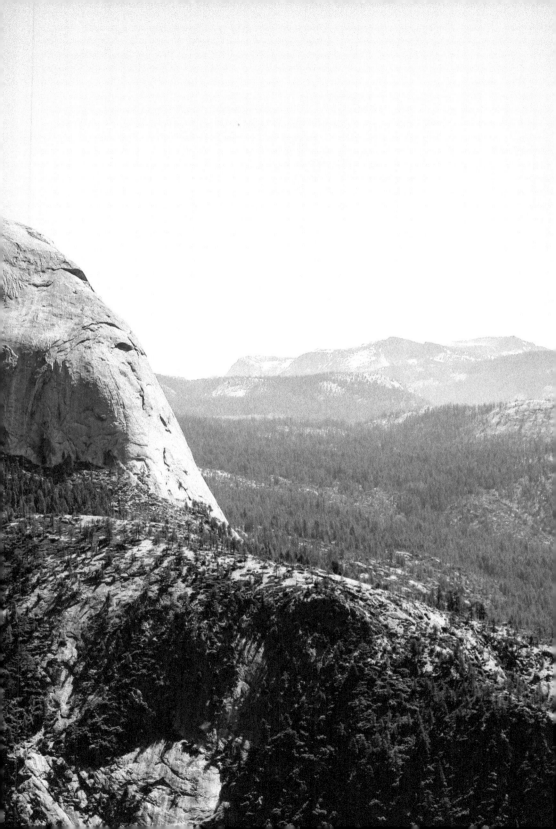

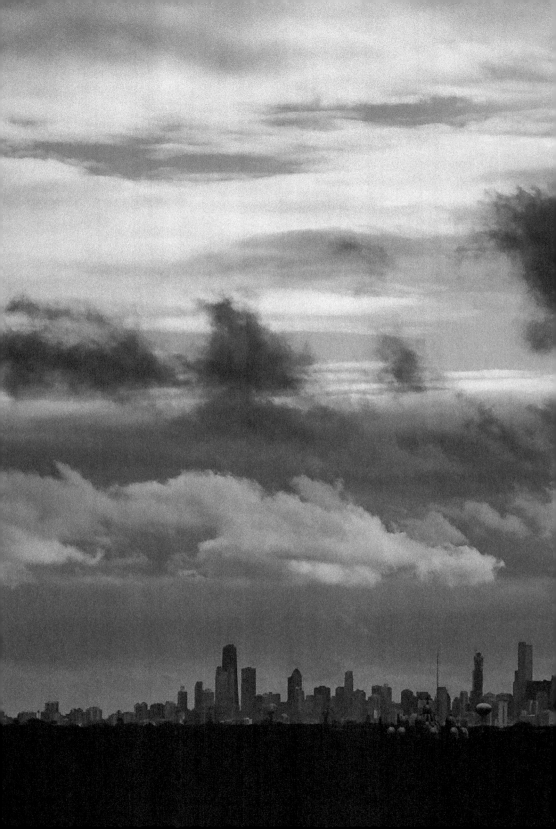

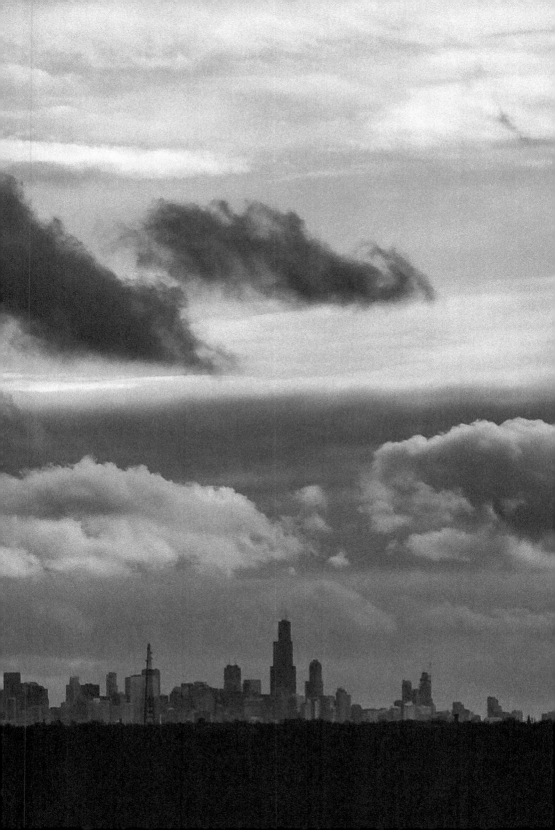

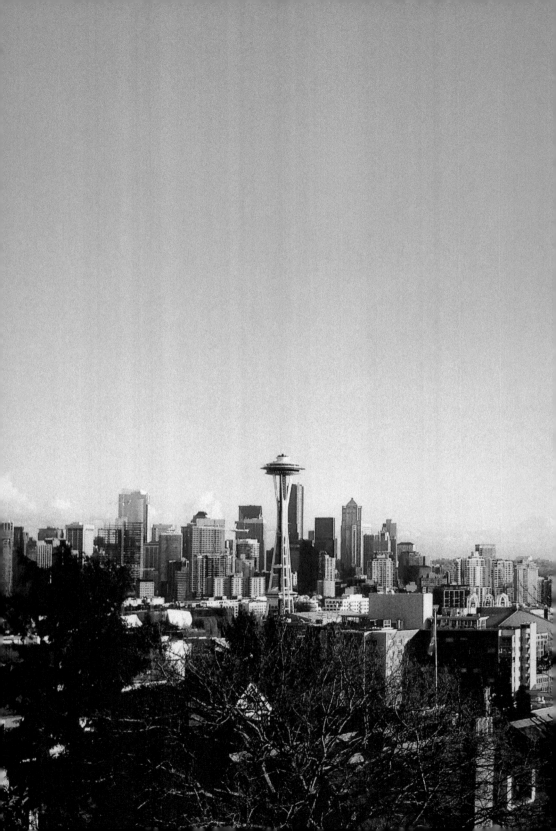

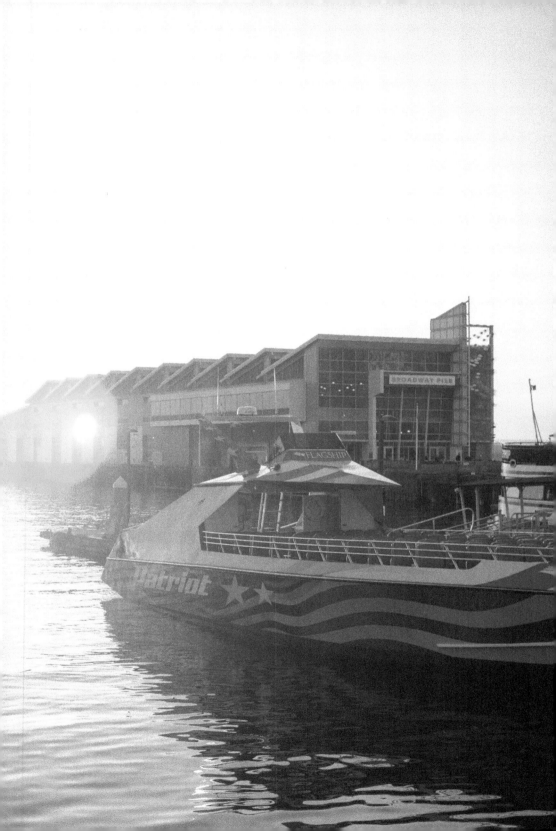

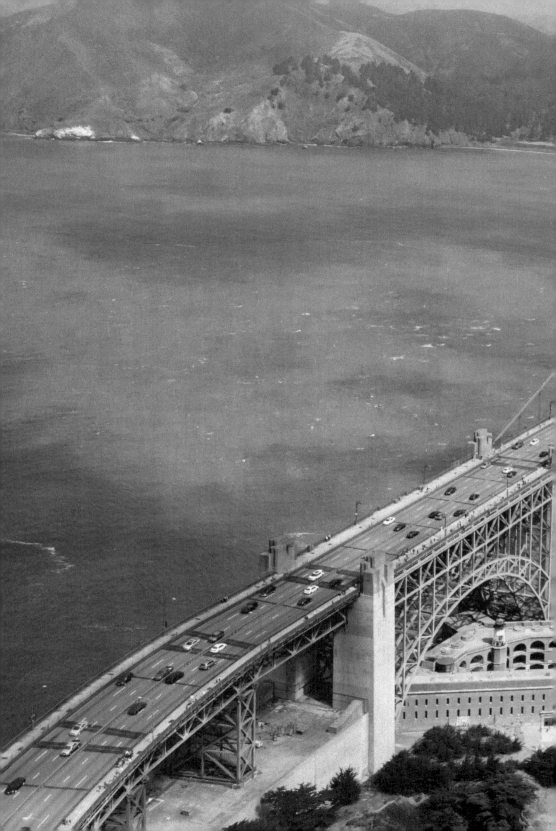

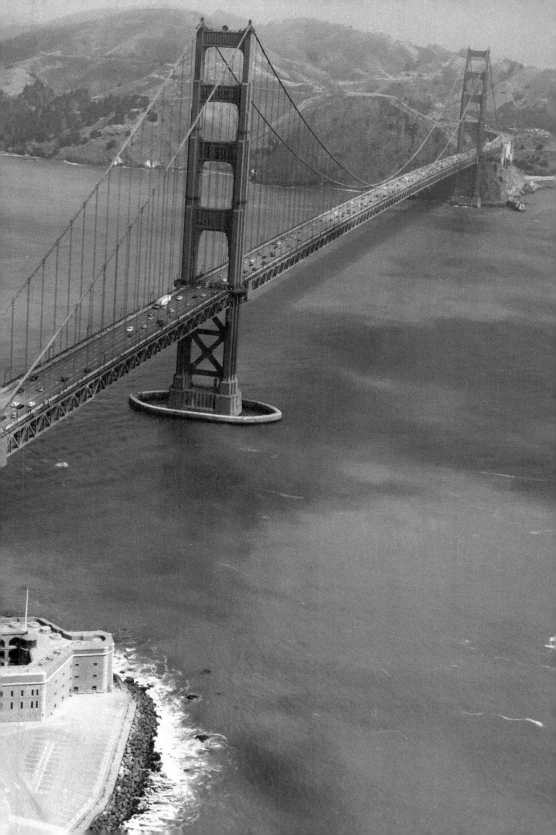

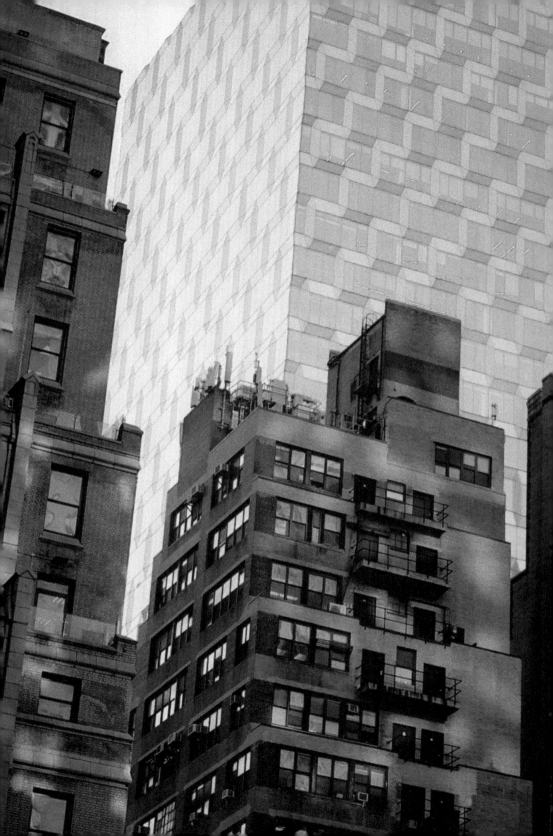

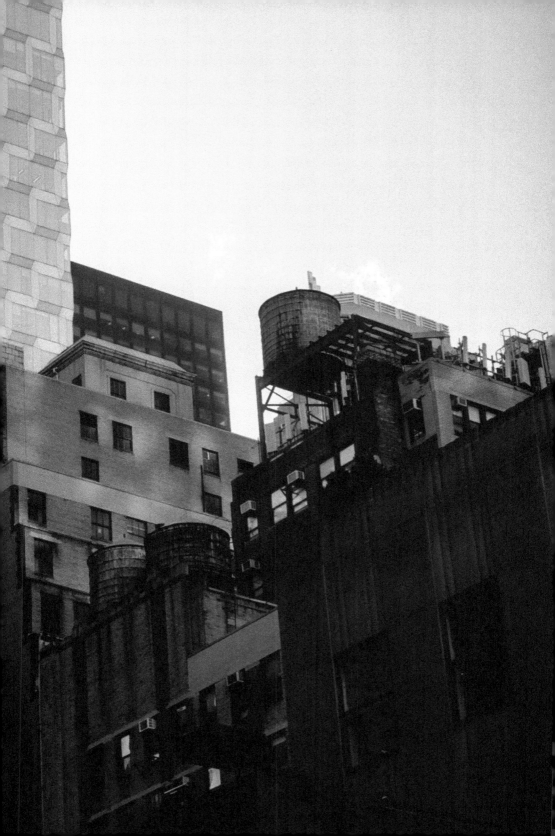

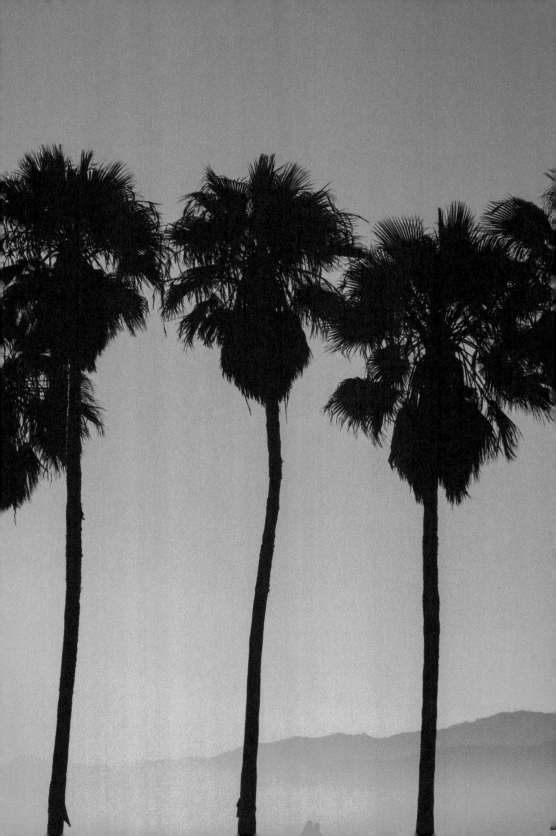

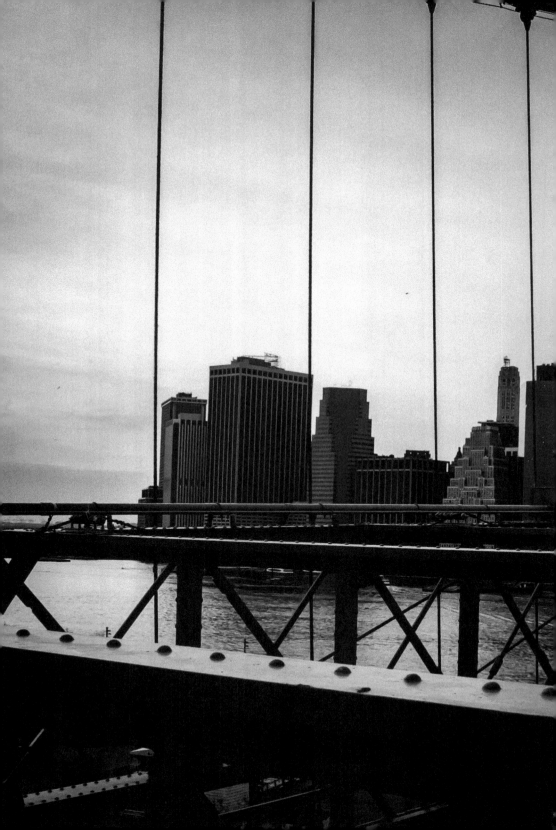

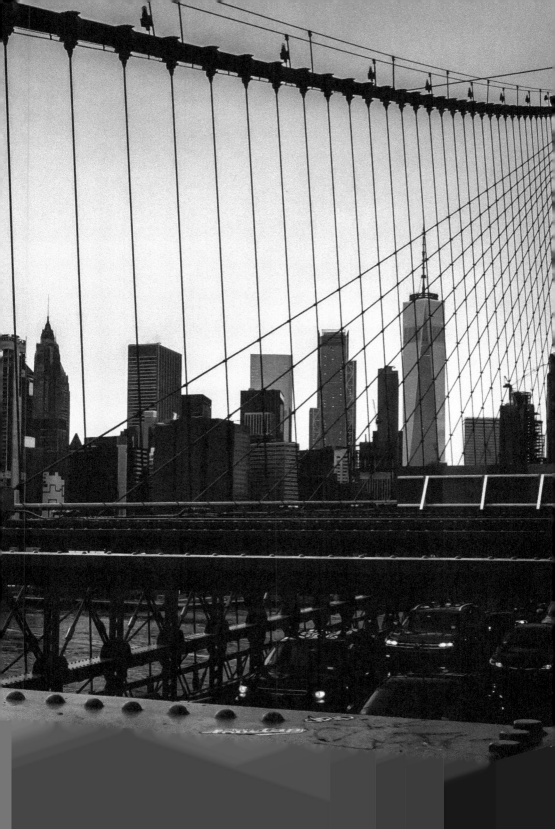

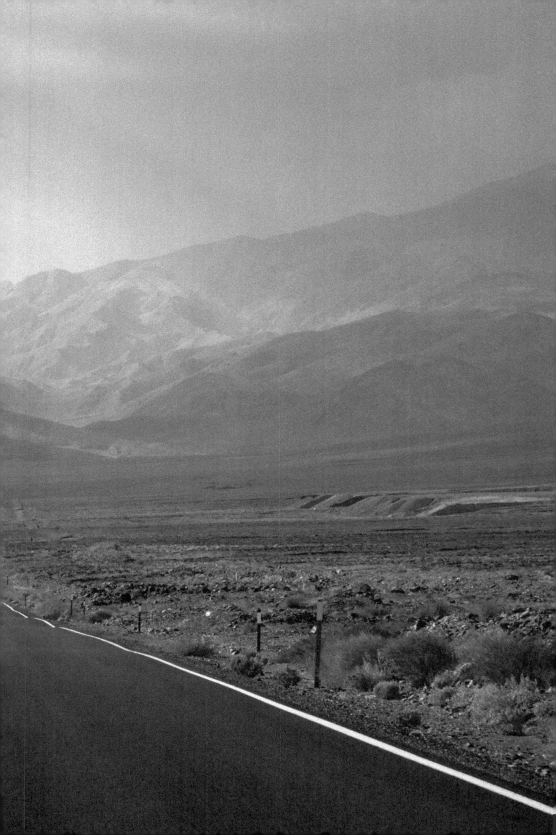

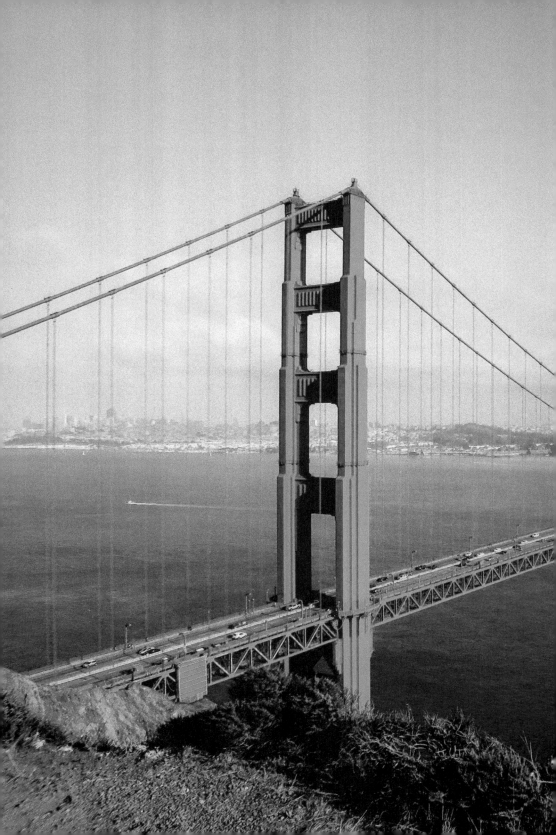

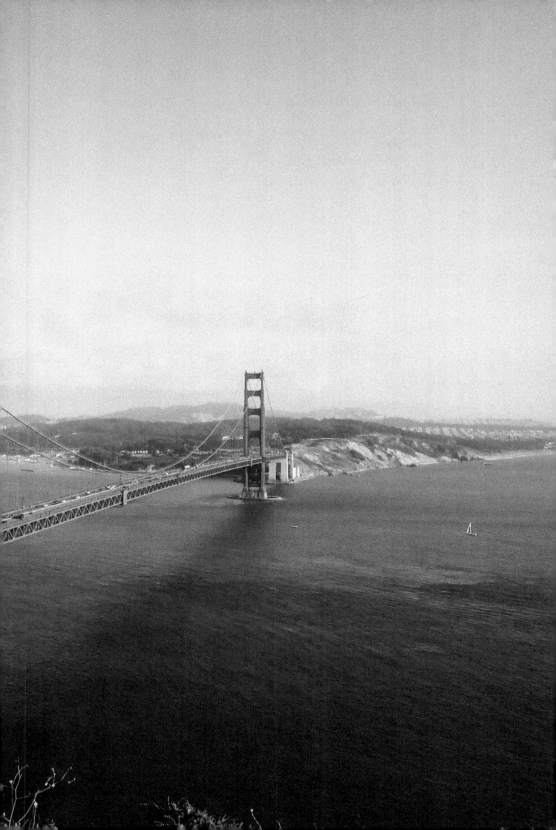

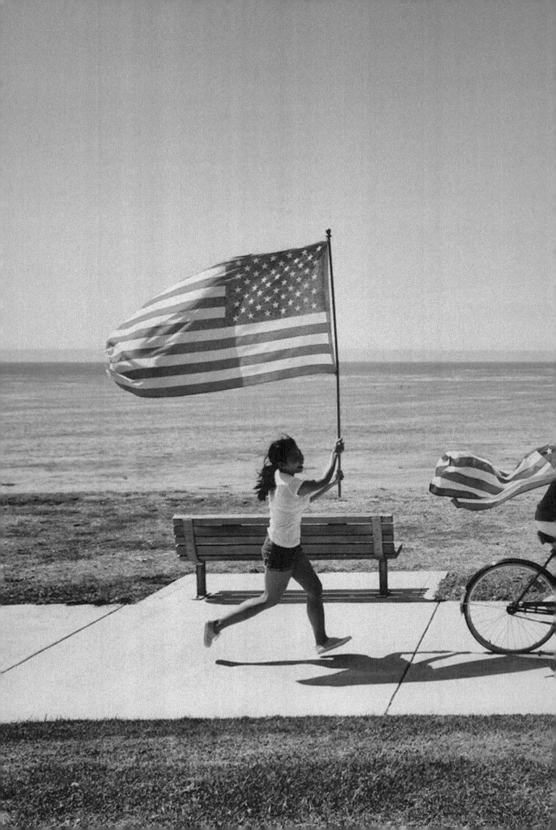

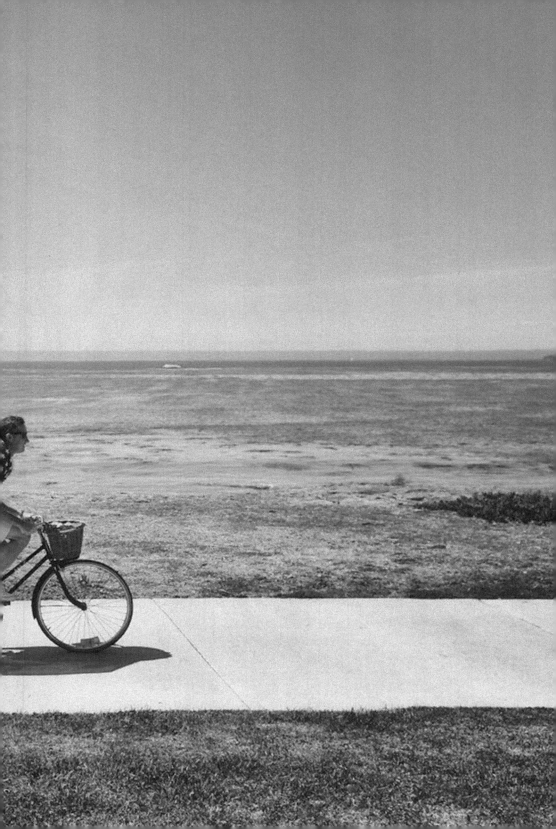

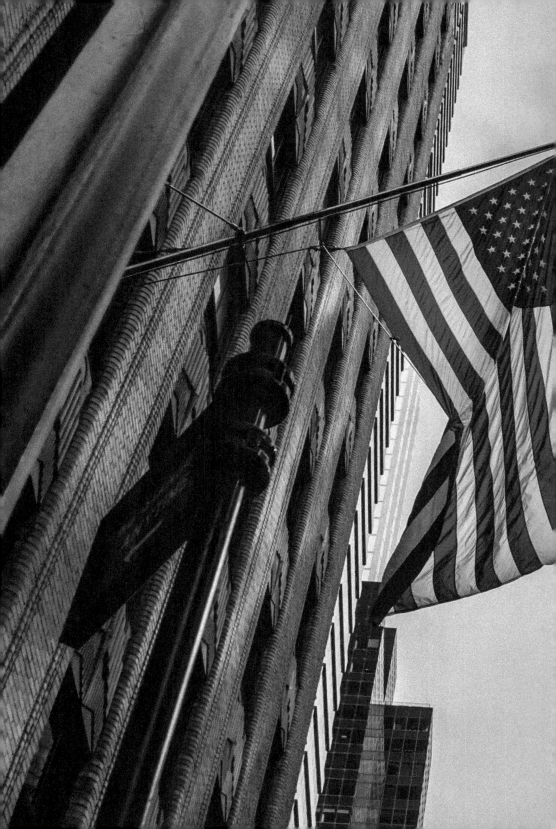

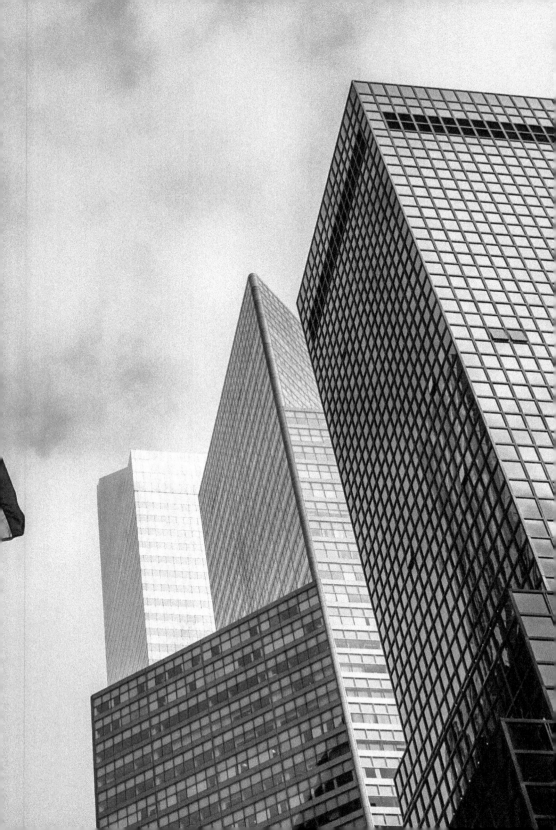

CPSIA information can be obtained
at www.ICGtesting.com
Printed in the USA
BVHW060824200519
548790BV00019B/1181/P